LECTURES ON SOME POINTS
IN THE HISTORY OF

# INDIAN BUDDHISM

# LECTURES ON SOME POINTS IN THE HISTORY OF

# INDIAN BUDDHISM

## (*The Hibbert Lectures*)

T. W. RHYS DAVIDS

GYAN

*Published by*

GYAN

Gyan Publishing House
5, Ansari Road
Daryaganj, New Delhi-110002
Phone: 011-47034999, 9811692060
E-mail: books@gyanbooks.com

*Distribution Network*
gyanbooks.com
India, USA, Canada, UK, Australia, France



ISBN : 978-81-212-2566-3 (HB)
First Published, 1881

2nd Impression 2020

*Printed at:* Gyan Press, Delhi.



**Lectures on Some Points in the History of Indian Buddhism**
Author: T. W. Rhys Davids

TO MY DEAR FATHER,

IN GRATEFUL AND LOVING REMEMBRANCE

OF

COUNSEL, HELP AND SYMPATHY.

# TABLE OF CONTENTS.

## LECTURE I.

### THE PLACE OF BUDDHISM IN THE DEVELOPEMENT OF RELIGIOUS THOUGHT

## Lecture II

## THE PĀLI PIṬAKAS.



## Lecture III.

## THE BUDDHIST THEORY OF KARMA.

Lecture IV

## BUDDHIST LIVES OF THE BUDDHA.

## Lecture V

## GOTAMA'S ORDER



## Lecture VI.

## LATER FORMS OF BUDDHISM.

## APPENDIX

## LECTURE I.

# THE PLACE OF BUDDHISM IN THE DEVELOPEMENT OF RELIGIOUS THOUGHT.

---

### Right and Wrong Uses of the Comparative Study of Religious Beliefs.

IT would be a hopeless task to attempt in six Lectures, that is to say, in six hours, to give any adequate account of that great movement which has influenced the greater portion of the human race during the lapse of so many centuries. It is therefore matter for congratulation that the task allotted to us is a much lighter one,—to discuss those points in the history of Buddhism which appear likely to throw light on the origin and growth of religious belief. This means, as I understand it, the origin and growth of religion outside, as well as inside, the circle of the Buddhist beliefs themselves. What we have to do is, in a word, to apply a particular method, the comparative method, to the study of the facts revealed to us by the history of Buddhism.

There is indeed a way of comparing religions one with another which leads to mere truisms, or even to erroneous conclusions. It is not uncommon, even now, to find such comparisons made with the object of evoking interest in other religions than our own, by showing that they teach some things which are also held among us. The Singhalese have an epithet which they apply in good-humoured sarcasm to Europeans, and which means "fellows with hats, hat fellows" (Toppi-kārayo). These fellows with the hats, and eighty-ton guns, and other signs of artistic and spiritual pre-eminence, are sometimes gifted with a sublime and admirable self-complacency which leads them to be surprised when they find fundamental truths of morality, or good sense in philosophy, taught among peoples who are not white and who go bare-headed. And being thus surprised, they are led to produce any evidence of such things, as if they were remarkable and interesting phenomena.

I beg to deprecate very strongly the study of other religions than our own merely to find out points on which we can agree with them; in other words, for it usually comes to that, the habit of judging of other religions by the degree of resemblance they bear to our own beliefs. There are ideas in Buddhism, no doubt, with which we can heartily sympathize; but the most instructive points in the history of that, or of any other religion, are often those with which we can least agree. The fact that truth can be found among all peoples and in all creeds, has been acknowledged through so many centuries by men eminent in the Church and out of it, that it has become almost a truism, and needs scarcely to be stated, certainly not to be proved.

---

For such purposes, comparisons are no longer of any service; and they will be of worse than no service if we imagine that likeness is any proof of direct relationship, that similarity of ideas in different countries shows that either the one or the other was necessarily a borrower. We can easily understand how Clement of Alexandria found in coincidences between Christian and pagan belief convincing evidence that the whole of the wisdom of the world (as he knew it) was borrowed from the Scriptures of his own faith. His was at least both a more liberal and a truer explanation of the facts than that other theory of the Jesuit father, who is related to have been so struck with the similarities between the Tibetan and the Roman ritual, that he thought the devil had deluded those unfortunate people with a blasphemous imitation of the religion of Christ.[1] It would of course be going too far to

[1] 1 Cor x 20, "They sacrifice to devils and not to God,' may have suggested the idea. The Spaniard Acosta, quoted in Lord Kingsborough's Antiquities of Mexico, Vol. vi. p 410, advances a similar explanation of the Mexican ritual.

deny that coincidences of belief are occasionally produced by actual contact of mind with mind; but it is no more necessary to assume that they always are so, than to suppose that chalk cliffs, if there be such, in China are produced by chalk cliffs in the Downs of Sussex. They have no connection one with another, except that both are the result of similar causes. Yet this method of reasoning is constantly found, not only through the whole range of the literature of the subject from classical times downwards, but even in works of the present day.

---

There is yet another use of the comparative study of religious beliefs, often hitherto, and still unfortunately, resorted to, against which we must be sedulously on our guard. One of the clearest statements of the doctrine I refer to may be found in a speech, most remarkable in many ways, delivered in our own House of Commons by a Member whose name has not been preserved, a "gentleman from Gray's Inn," in the year 1530. The date is significant, for the idea of religious freedom, or even of religious toleration, was then almost unknown.[1]

[1] Unknown, that is, among Christians Complete toleration, as is well known, is one of the most fundamental teachings of Buddhism, and was laid down as a duty in edicts recorded on stone two centuries and a half before the birth of Christ This is so striking that I quote these edicts in full in the Appendix.

*Colossal Avalokitesvara-Padmapani: Nalanda*
c. 800 or 900 A.D.

Rail pillar; Cross-bar, Middle Phase: Amaravati

Stone, standing Buddha, Gupta period, from India (Brit. Mus.)

*Bodhisattva Vajrapani: Indian Museum; Calcutta*, 1100—1200 A.D.

*Standing Buddha; Bronze: Nalanda, early 900* A.D.

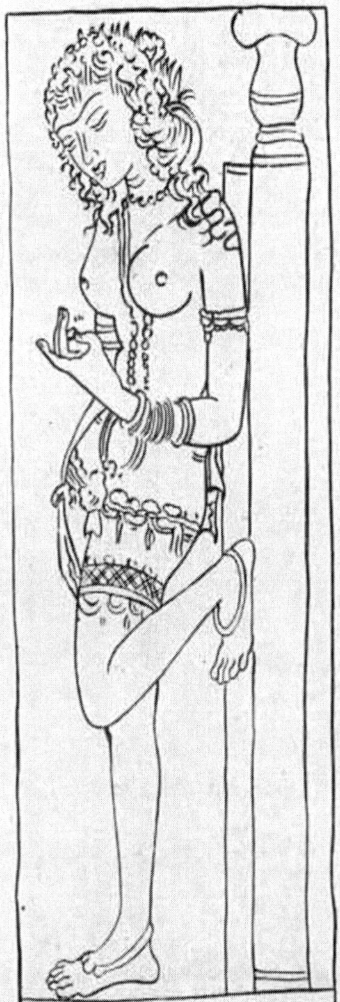

"The Wanton Lady",
Cave XVII, Visvantara Jataka,
Ajanta c. 650 A.D.

*Jewellery from Sculptures at Barhut*

Part of the inner face of the North Torana. Sanchi, Early 1st Century B.C.

*Bodhisattva from Fondukistan; Musee Guimet, Paris*

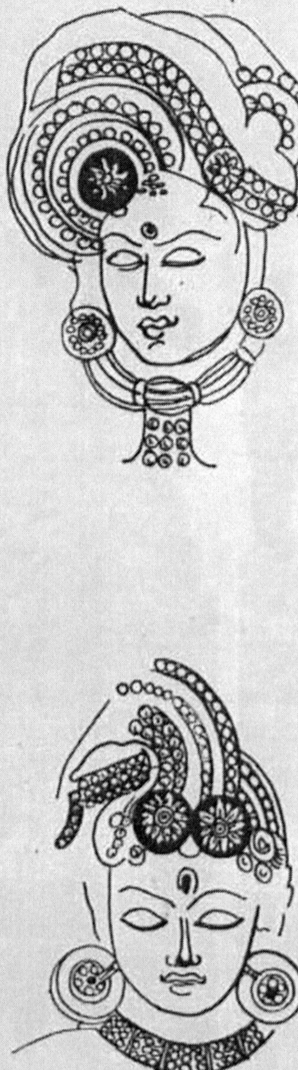

*Ornamental Head-Dress: Figures in Bhaja Caves*
*(1st Century A.D.)*

"Mr. Speaker," said this barrister, "if none else "but the Bishop of Rochester or his adherents did hold "this language, it would less trouble me. But since "so many religious and different sects, now conspicuous "in the whole world, do not only vindicate unto them-"selves the name of the True Church, but labour be-"twixt invitations and threats for nothing less than "to make us resign our faith to a simple obedience, I "shall crave leave to propose what I think fit in this "case for us laiques and secular persons to do. . . . .

"For as several teachers, not only differing in lan-"guage, habit and ceremony, or at least in some of "these, but peremptory and opposite in their doctrines, "do present themselves, much circumspection must be "used." . . . .

Then, after pointing out the difficulty of choosing between these "several teachers," the gentleman from Gray's Inn proposes that

". . . . he [the laique] shall hold himself to common, "authentic, and universal truths; and consequently "inform himself what, in the several articles proposed "to him, is so taught as it is first written in the heart, "and together delivered in all the laws and religions "he can hear of in the whole world; this certainly can "never deceive him." . . . .

If this plan of arriving at truth be followed, "it will "concern our several teachers to initiate us in this "(universally accepted) doctrine before they come to "any particular doctrine, lest otherwise they do like "those who would persuade us to renounce daylight "to study only by their candle." . . . .

The gentleman from Gray's Inn then sets out what he thought to be such universally accepted beliefs, and concludes: "These therefore, as universal and un-"doubted truths, should in my opinion be first received. "They will at least keep us from impiety and atheism. ". . . . Let us therefore establish and fix these catholic "and universal notions: . . . . so that whether the "Eastern, Western, Northern or Southern teachers—"and particularly whether my lord Rochester, Luther, "Eccius, Zwinglius, Erasmus, Melanchthon, &c.—be "in the right, we laiques may so build upon these "catholic and infallible grounds of religion, as what-"soever superstructure of faith be raised, these foun-"dations yet may support them."

The speaker—evidently a man of rare toleration and enlightenment—was a Catholic, and his speech is really nothing else but the Quod semper, quod ubique, quod ab omnibus, of the Catholic Church applied in a way which would have put an end at once to the bitter feelings and useless persecutions which so lamentably disgraced the eventful struggle then already commencing to shake thrones and peoples. His view has also much in common with another well-known adage, Vox populi vox Dei; and if the "gentle-"man from Gray's Inn" had been speaking only of elementary morals, one might go a long way with him. But in matters of religious belief it is scarcely ever the majority of men, far less all men, who are usually right. On the contrary, the minorities have time on their side; and it is no argument, for instance, for the truth of the Buddhist theory that it has always been professed by a larger number of people than the Christian. Among the most "universal and catholic beliefs" have been an unquestioning faith in witchcraft and astrology; though an influential minority of mankind has now finally rejected them both. It is quite open to argument that we may go so far as to say that whatsoever has been universally believed among men, in matters of religion, is probably false. One of the many modern writers who follow the method we are discussing, says plausibly enough that he desires to combine "the testimony rendered by man's spiritual faculties in different epochs and races concerning questions on which these faculties are of necessity the final appeal."[1] But the facts surely show that the testimony has been more often wrong than right. However valuable the combination, or the comparison, of this testimony may be for historical purposes, it will disclose to us no infallible guide concealed behind the veil of multiform error. "I must think," says Dr. Legge, "that the comparative study of religions will

[1] Johnson, Oriental Religions India, Vol. i. p 2

"dissipate this imagination, and prove it to be an "unsubstantial hope."[1] Surely that is the correct view. And in any case, we shall not here conduct our inquiries with any such object, with any such hope. The task of the historian of religious belief is a much humbler one, simply to ascertain, if he can, the process by which men have come to believe as they do.

---

These, then, being methods and objects which we shall endeavour not to follow or to seek, what is the purpose which a comparison of Buddhism with other religions may reasonably be expected to serve?

An illustration will perhaps make this clear. In the allied science of comparative philology, we find, firstly, that words in the more modern dialects of any family are derived, as far as possible historically, from words or roots in the older dialects; and, secondly, that general rules respecting the tendencies of the growth of language, and of vowel and consonantal change, are laid down as being of very general or even sometimes of universal application. It is quite true that (owing to the fact that only one branch of the subject—the Āryan branch—has been, as yet, at all completely worked out) most of the general rules or tendencies as

[1] Religions of China, p 287

yet discovered, either depend upon facts observed in, or are applicable only to, the Āryan field of language. Comparative philologists may have been too much given, perhaps, to regarding all questions of the science of language from an exclusively Āryan standpoint. But some progress has already been made in the observation of tendencies which hold good among words and families of speech not related to one another. And it is precisely such general observations which are now, and will increasingly be, the most valuable results of philological research.

So also in comparative mythology. Who has not been charmed by the clear and unexpected light thrown from the poetry of the Vedas upon many of the myths most familiar to us in the literature of Greece and Rome? But myths are not confined to the shores of the Mediterranean. Much of this curious phase of belief that is found there and elsewhere cannot be similarly explained by derivation from Vedic or other hymns. Even when it can, the difficulty has only been removed one stage further back. And the most valuable results of the study of comparative mythology depend upon the observation of those general tendencies which prevail in the growth of early beliefs of this kind common among men.

In the same way it is such general tendencies as a right use of the comparative study of religious belief will enable us to observe, which will be the most valuable results of our inquiries.

---

We must not hope, however, to find more than tendencies, to find laws in the scientific sense. The expression "Science of Religion" may be useful as a short phrase in which to sum up, or include, all our knowledge concerning religious beliefs. But if it be intended to suggest that we have yet found, or can ever hope to find, such fixed rules in these matters as are laid down in the exact sciences, the expression Science of Religion must be admitted to be a misnomer. As the word science is most naturally and immediately referred to the exact sciences, it is unfortunate, to say the least, to talk as yet of a Science of Religion; and the name will scarcely be appropriate till the word science has changed or enlarged its connotation. On the other hand, too, no generally accepted opinion is more fallacious than the frequently repeated dictum that "human nature is everywhere the same." Most especially on that side of their nature which we are here discussing, the religious side, men's nature differs greatly according to their different history, their different surroundings, their different education. It is only under similar conditions that man's nature can be everywhere similar; and it is chiefly because those conditions are never precisely the same, that it is impossible to lay down any hard and fast rules of the developement (or the decay, as some prefer—it does not matter which) of religious beliefs.

---

Such being some of the cautions, as to both aim and method, which we ought carefully to bear in mind when comparing the details of Buddhism with those of other systems, we should also never lose sight of the true position of Buddhism in the general religious history of India and of the world at large.

Buddhism is one of the so-called "book religions." When we hear that it was founded some five hundred years before the birth of Christ, we are apt to think that it is very old,—as old, as primitive, as rudimentary, as the arts and sciences of those far-off times. But, comparatively speaking, it is one of the very latest products of the human mind.

Our conceptions on this point are prone to be darkened by the shortness of the period that has elapsed since the dawn of recorded history. It is true that throughout the world recorded history can only be said to begin with any completeness about five hundred years before the Christian era. Here and there in isolated places we have documentary evidence of the history of some few tribes for a period somewhat earlier.

And from the oldest of these sources, and from still older documents that are not historical, we can conjecture, with more or less accuracy, certain general facts concerning the history, for some still previous centuries, of those races among whom those sources were handed down. But aback of all these there stretches the long vista of unknown centuries which must form the background of the picture in which Buddhism should be presented to our minds, if we wish that picture to be drawn in true perspective.

Compared with what had been before the rise of Buddhism, the distance between ourselves and it vanishes away to insignificance; and the first thing we have to do is to attempt as best we can to realize to ourselves the long developement of which it was the logically ultimate outcome, and, in a sense, the close.

It is to be regretted that exigencies of time and space prevent this part of our subject being treated with anything like the extent which its importance demands. And all the more so, since the difficulty of the problem and the incertitude of our knowledge prevent the little that can be said from being said sharply and clearly. But it would add considerably to our difficulties in the subsequent part of this course, if no foundation had been laid for our historical sketch by a description, however slight, of the growth of those ideas among which Buddhism was born.

Many centuries before the time of our earliest records, the parent race of the seven Āryan races—the Hindūs, Persians, Greeks, Romans, Kelts, Teutons and Sklaves—had passed through the earliest phases of its religious beliefs.

Attempts have been made with considerable success to argue from the words and beliefs found, in their earliest records, to have been common afterwards among one or more of the seven races, to the religious ideas which must have existed in the parent stock. Made with due caution, such inferences are fair. At the time when their earliest records were composed, there was no likelihood of any direct borrowing between the several races, and the results are confirmed by our knowledge of early religious beliefs elsewhere.

It is sufficient for our purpose that the beliefs of the remote ancestors of the Buddhists may be summed up as having resulted from that curious attitude of mind which is now designated by the word Animism. They had come to believe, most probably through the influence of dreams, in the existence of souls, or ghosts, or spirits, inside their own bodies; and they had not yet learned to discriminate in this respect between themselves and the other animals and objects around them which seemed to be possessed of powei and movement. The Vedas, though they are oui earliest records, show us only a very advanced stage in the beliefs resulting from this simple and unquestioning faith, so widely diffused among all races and ages of mankind. The more powerful spirits or ghosts supposed to dwell in various external things, have already become in the Vedas objects of greater fear than the rest; they are endowed with higher attributes, are surrounded by deeper mystery, and have been promoted to be kings, as it were, among the gods. These were chiefly the spirits supposed to animate the sky and the heavenly bodies; and the promotion of these spirits had so dimmed the comparative glory of the rest, that the Animism had become in the Vedas what we call Polytheism.

But the newer stage of belief was no contradiction of the older; it was simply a further advance along the same lines, and resting on the same foundations. The lesser spirits, or at least most of them, survived as naiads and dryads, spirits of the streams and trees, demons, goblins, ogres, spirit-messengers, and fairies, good or bad. And the old belief in mysteriously animated objects survived, too, in the belief in magic, in sorcery, and in charms of various kinds.

And here it may be pointed out that it is claiming too much for the Rig Veda to maintain that it has preserved for us the whole of the ancient Indian thought on theological matters. Precisely because the lesser spirits had become, comparatively speaking, of less account, because each one of them was believed in and feared by fewer mortals, we must expect to find them less mentioned and less described in the collection of the hymns to the supposed greater spirits. But the less important beliefs played on the whole a perhaps greater part in the actual daily thoughts of most of the ordinary men of the Āryan tribes; and we must complete the picture by the invaluable details preserved in the Atharva Veda, and also elsewhere surviving in the later literature.

---

With regard to the internal spirits, the souls of men, the old Āryans believed that the soul survived after the body, which enclosed it, had passed away. They feared and worshipped the ghosts of departed ancestors, and did not realize as possible or probable any cessation of the life they expected beyond the grave. The good and brave and liberal enjoyed a new life of happiness in that new and spiritual body to which the ghost of the deceased changed or developed (or perhaps, for the point is not quite clear, which was inhabited by the spirit) after death. Whether they clearly held that the future life was never-ending, whether the belief in immortality was actually held by all, is very doubtful. There is all the difference between thinking of a future life without raising the question of its duration, and firmly believing that it would never end. But at least some of the more highly gifted, the more ardent among the later Vedic poets, looked after death for an immortal life of sensual bliss.[1] On the other hand, the bad, the false, the stingy, enter into the nethermost deep of darkness. Of a life before this one, or of a return of the soul to this world, either as man or animal, there seems to have then been no suspicion; though there are one or two late passages which suggest the possibility of a departed spirit being recalled to life and to security here on earth.[2]

---

In their most essential elements these ideas of the future life were not only Vedic, they were the common inheritance of the seven Āryan races; they were retained among the Persians—the brother-race of the Hindūs—in a form strengthened, no doubt, and altered on the same lines, but very little modified by opposing conceptions. And when we find that the oldest Hebrew books show little trace of that belief in an immortal future life which became so common among the Jews after the captivity in Mesopotamia, and that no other Semitic tribes seem to have originated the idea, the question springs spontaneously to one's mind, whether we have not met, in these ancient Āryan beliefs, with

---

1 Rig Veda ix. 113, 7—11, Atharva Veda iv 34, 2—4, and other passages, quoted in Muir's Sanskrit Texts, Vol v. pp 306 foll.

2 Rig Veda x 58, 1, x. 60, 10, loc cit p 313

the foundation-stone of a far-spreading edifice, of that all-powerful belief in the immortality of the soul which has played so mighty a part in the influences which have shaped the Europe of to-day.

---

But in India, through the following centuries, there was gradually, very gradually, brought about a curious change in these fundamental articles of religious belief. When Buddhism arose, the accepted and general belief was that the souls of men had previously existed inside the bodies of other men, or gods, or animals, or had animated material objects; and that when they left the bodies they now inhabited, they would enter upon a new life, of a like temporary nature, under one or other of these various individual forms—the particular form being determined by the goodness or evil of the acts done in the present existence. Life, therefore, was held to be a never-ending chain, a never-ending struggle. For however high the conditions to which any soul had attained, it was liable, by one act of wickedness, or even of carelessness, to fall again into one or other of the miserable states.

There was a hopelessness about this creed in direct contrast to the childlike fulness of hope, the strong desire for life, that is so clearly revealed in the Vedas. Very probably the great mass of the people, occupied in their daily duties, their worldly hopes and fears, did not allow themselves to be much influenced by this new creed of transmigration; but the more their attention was drawn to religious matters—and at some crisis or another of his life this may have happened to most of them—a vague feeling of helplessness and hopelessness must have obtained the mastery over them.

---

A way of escape had indeed been found. A modification of the theory of external spirits had pointed the way to this new refuge for the internal spirit, for each man's soul or self. There were too many earnest and intellectual minds among the then Hindus for Polytheism, tempered only by a subservient Animism, to remain supreme. As among the Jews and among the Greeks, so also among the Hindūs, there were not a few to whom a unity underlying the many personified forms of external nature became gradually more and more visible. Among the Jews, the corresponding belief—the belief in one God—had already, about the time of the rise of Buddhism, gained a complete hold of the general population. Among the Greeks, the belief in ὁ Θεός, or rather in a τὸ Θεῖον, as distinct from the belief in οἱ Θεόι, in Deity as distinct from the older deities, was confined mostly to those educated in, or under the immediate influence of, the schools of philosophy. And so in the valley of the Ganges, it was only in the schools of the philosophizing ascetics, mostly but by no means exclusively Brāhmans, that a unity, not indeed a personal God in the modern sense, but a neuter, cold and passionless First Cause, was conceived to be the source, the abiding support, of all phenomena.

---

In speaking of these later beliefs, so nearly related to our own, it is difficult to make use of terms not liable to much misconception. It has been maintained that the Jewish belief in an Evil Spirit, side by side with the Great Spirit, and in subordinate angels and archangels, good and bad, is sufficient to render inaccurate any description of them as Monotheists. It is probable that few, if any, of the Grecian thinkers believed in the existence of one external Spirit only, to the complete exclusion of all minor deities. And certainly even the most advanced among the pre-Buddhistic Hindus never became what would now be called pure Theists.

They could better be called Pantheists; but even this expression can only be used of them in a sense not applicable to the followers of the Pantheism which has grown out of Christian theology or Greek philosophy. The Indian philosophers continued to believe in the souls or spirits supposed to exist inside the human body, and in all the hierarchy of the external spirits, the gods of rivers, trees and pools, of earth and sky and sea, and all their numerous progeny. But they held all these, and all matter, to be the mere sportive emanations of a supreme primordial Spirit, who was unconscious, and who was led by causes beyond his (or rather its) control to manifest itself in all those temporary and changing forms which make up this world and its inhabitants. All things are unreal. All being, save the One, is evanescent. And as to the souls of men, though they are condemned to wander for ever and ever from shape to shape, from labour to trouble, their existence is not independent; they are not self-existent, and they can defeat the unlucky action of the God that gave birth to their individuality by certain ceremonies, or a certain kind of knowledge, held, by various opposing schools, to be able to destroy again that individuality by bringing about the return of the spark to the central fire, by the absorption of the human soul in that Great Soul which was supposed to be the only real existence.

Can any of the many different speculations which have grown up in Christian soil be said to be the same as this hopeless creed? Can these Indian notions be accurately described or correctly summed up by any of our Western names? We may admit that the general course of speculation has run along parallel lines in the valley of the Ganges and in the basin of the Mediterranean. But modern Pantheism has arisen after the stage of those polytheistic beliefs of which Indian Pantheism was the outgrowth and the explanation: and European Pantheism, whether Greek, mediæval or modern, is always, or very nearly always, entirely uninfluenced—I may venture to say, untarnished—by the longing to escape from life. If we, then, use the words Pantheism or Monotheism when describing Hindu thought, we should never forget that, though similar in many respects, they are yet quite as different in other respects from the Pantheisms and Monotheisms of the West.

---

In this curious despair of life, we must, I think, admit the power of an influence the very existence of which it has become the fashion to deny. Mr. Buckle may have wished to push the influence of climate too far, to regard it too much as an explanation sufficient of itself. But when we find this despair of life conspicuously absent not only in the Vedas, but in the earliest records of the other Āryan races, and in all the schemes of life that have obtained currency in more temperate climes, we cannot omit to notice the fact that it sprang up in India after the Āryan tribes had descended into the valley of the Ganges, and had been long under the influence of the oppressive heat to which they had not been accustomed, and from which there was no escape. It is true that World-weariness, Weltschmerz, is not unknown in Europe. But the fact that it has arisen mostly at a certain period of life shows it to be here also at least in part due to physical causes. Few individuals in temperate climes are permanently pessimists; and such pessimist philosophy as does exist is more theoretical than practical, and has never obtained so complete a hold of all the more thoughtful minds as it had in India at the time of the rise of Buddhism.

---

It is possible to argue that this weariness of life was due to the system of caste, a yoke which seems intolerable to modern European minds. But the evils of the system are often exaggerated, the immutability of its rules is often overstated; and in those early times, when the system was only arriving at complete developement, it is probable that the people themselves by no means felt its yoke so heavy as it is commonly supposed to be.

As is now well known, there is no mention of caste in the oldest hymns of the Vedas. But the bitter contempt of the Āryans for foreign tribes, their domineering and intolerant spirit, their strong antipathies of race and of religion, are in harmony with the special features of caste as afterwards established. It is natural that, as the bitter struggles against the non-Āryan peoples died away, the domineering spirit of the conquerors should have lasted on, and have found vent for itself in the pride of class distinctions. It is accordingly only in some of the latest Vedic hymns that we find the first mention of those four classes—the Brāhmans, the Rājanyas, the Vaisyas and the Ṣudras—to which all the later castes have been subsequently traced back. Even then the division was as yet into classes, not into castes properly so called. And it is in the Brāhmana literature that we come to the earliest passages in which exclusive privileges are claimed for the Brāhmans as priests, and for the nobles as entitled to receive the sacred unction. It seems certain that when the Brāhmanas were first composed the barrier between all the higher classes had become impassable, or, in other words, that these classes had been hardened into castes.

It is most probable that this momentous step followed upon, and was chiefly due to the previous establishment of, a similar hard and fast line preventing any one belonging to the non-Āryan tribes from intermarrying with an Āryan family, or being incorporated into the Āryan race It was the hereditary disability the Āryans had succeeded in imposing upon races they despised, which, re-acting within their own circle, and strengthened by the very intolerance that gave it birth, has borne such bitter fruit through so many centuries But it is perhaps scarcely surprising that the pride of race should have put an impassable barrier between the warlike Āryans and the darker races whom they had conquered in so many fights. It is no isolated fact that pride of birth had led the nobles to separate themselves from the mass of the people. It is not in India alone that the superstitious fears of all have yielded to the priesthood an unquestioned and profitable supremacy. And there are proofs enough of the tendency of occupations, in the earlier stages of civilization, to become hereditary.

The state of society in the valley of the Ganges at the time of the rise of Buddhism, was not so very different from the state of society in other races at similar stages of their history. The hereditary priesthood, the exclusive privileges of the Brāhmans, were, no doubt, as incontestable as the hereditary priesthood and exclusive privileges of the corresponding classes in Judæa in the time of Christ. Superstitions regarding purity and impurity, which play so great a part elsewhere in the settlement of early religious and social customs, were held as strongly as among the Jews and Persians. And a few, but by no means all or the most important, of men's daily occupations had become confined to certain families, which were really castes in the modern sense. The larger divisions into classes had also already merged into castes; intermarriages were no longer possible except between equal ranks. No Kshatriya could any longer become a Brāhman, far less one of the aboriginal tribes enter into the social ranks of the sacred

Āryans. But the elaborate distinctions of the modern castes were then unknown; the stringent penalties, which in after times followed on the breach of caste rules, had not yet been heard of; and the commonest modes of livelihood, agriculture and trade, were followed, even more indiscriminately than now, by all alike.

---

The worst part of the circle of caste ideas was undoubtedly the supremacy accorded to the Brāhmans by birth. But even this might have caused little practical harm had it not been for the soul-theory, and for the curious belief in the efficacy of the rites and ceremonies they could perform, on which that supremacy rested. These beliefs, perhaps a necessary, certainly an almost universal stage in the developement of religion, had a most baleful influence on the every-day life of the people among whom Buddhism was first proclaimed. The power of the gods was to them a very real thing. The influence of the stars, and the good or ill luck of the days on which the various customary ceremonies were to be performed, or the various businesses of life were to be set on foot, were to them of very real importance. There was indeed very little, if any, of what we should now call prayer. But the gods could be compelled by sacrifices rightly offered, by hymns properly intoned, to favour the fortunate worshipper;

and charms rightly recited, horoscopes correctly cast, talismans whose power had been already tested, could ensure the results which men had most at heart. The happiness of the soul, too, in its next birth depended upon the due performance of settled ceremonies; and for all these things the help of the Brāhmans was required, and had to be richly paid. It would be useless to attempt to disguise the evils resulting from such a state of things. But we should never forget that the evil was due, not to the depravity of the Brāhmans, but to the beliefs of the people; and that those beliefs were the natural outcome and result of the previous stages of belief through which they had passed during the long ages of their previous history.

---

Buddhism was by no means the first effort that had been made to change this condition of things. There was absolute freedom of thought in ancient India. The Brāhmans themselves were often the leaders in enunciating new views, which would elsewhere have been condemned as heterodox; and men of other castes were allowed to set up as teachers of systems really incompatible with the inherited beliefs. Invaluable records of this philosophical and sophistical tendency of the Brāhmans, to which some reference has already been made, is preserved in the Upanishads,—in many respects the most interesting portion of the literature of pre-Buddhistic India that has come down to us. And the lineal descendants of these schools of thought are the well-known six systems of Hindu philosophy, one of which, the Vedāntist, has acquired so deep an influence over all the later varieties of Hindu thought. Of the then opinions of the thinkers of other sects we have no records. But their descendants no doubt greatly influenced the later modifications of Buddhism, and the sect now called Jains has probably preserved the teachings of others.

One distinguished scholar, Professor Jacobi, has supposed that the Buddhist theory of the Buddhas was derived from a corresponding theory of the forerunners of the Jains; and it is common ground to many writers on the history of religion that Gotama borrowed largely from Kapila, the reputed founder of one of these early systems, the Sānkhya (or numeral) philosophy. But I would venture to enter a protest against such arguments. The extant books of the Jains are many centuries later than the Pāli Piṭakas. There is not the slightest evidence that any one of the writings of the six schools of philosophy are pre-Buddhistic. Such similarity as really exists between any of these works and the Pāli Piṭakas may perhaps be due to a common origin; it is quite as likely that the Buddhist ideas are the originals; and in any case it is to works known to exist before the time of Gotama, and especially to the earlier Upanishads, that we must look if we wish to discover what Indian philosophy really was before the advent of Buddhism.

---

Now unfortunately the Upanishads, by different authors and of different dates, are as difficult to appreciate and to understand as the earliest philosophers of the Greeks, and for a similar reason. They present to us, not a finished system, but the beginnings of thought, the vague struggles of earnest minds first grappling with the great problems of life. But one idea recurs throughout their long, and usually tedious, verbiage, and that is the belief that there was something far better, far higher, far more enduring, than the right performance of sacrifice; that the object of the wise man should be to know, inwardly and consciously, *the Great Soul of all; and that by this knowledge* his individual soul would become united to the Supreme Being, the true and absolute Self. This was the highest point of the old Indian philosophy; it was the ultimate outcome of the long history of the Āryan spirit-belief; and on those old lines, in that same direction, it is difficult to see what farther step was even possible.

The distinguishing characteristic of Buddhism was that it started on a new line, that it looked at the deepest questions men have to solve from an entirely different standpoint. It swept away from the field of its vision the whole of the great soul-theory which had hitherto so completely filled and dominated the minds of the superstitious and of the thoughtful alike. For the first time in the history of the world, it proclaimed a salvation which each man could gain for himself, and by himself, in this world, during this life, without any the least reference to God, or to gods, either great or small.

Like the Upanishads, it placed the first importance on knowledge; but it was no longer a knowledge of God, it was a clear perception of the real nature, as they supposed it to be, of men and things. And it added to the necessity of knowledge, the necessity of purity, of courtesy, of uprightness, of peace, and of a universal love, "far-reaching, grown great, and beyond measure."

The adherents of the new sect, as the Book of the Great Decease puts it, were to strive to be "full of "confidence, modest in heart, ashamed of wrong, full of "learning, strong in energy, active in mind, and full of "wisdom;" they were to "live in the practice, both in "public and private, of those virtues which, when "unbroken, intact, unspotted and unblemished, make "men free, and which are untarnished by the belief in "the efficacy of any outward acts of ritual or ceremony, "by the hope of any kind of future life"[1]

[1] See Rh D, Buddhist Suttas from the Pāli, pp 8, 10

We are not called upon here to attempt any estimate, or to come to any conclusion, as to whether this new departure was or was not right, much less whether it is the only right one. What I venture to submit to you is merely that it is this new departure, this ignoring of the soul, which is the most important fact in the comparative study of Buddhism. Everywhere where the attitude of mind called Animism—the first attempt at science, as it is the first step in religion, for these meet together at the birth, just as they will kiss each other at the close of history—everywhere where Animism has been permanently modified, it has been so by its developement into Polytheism; and this, though far from universal, is true not only of the seven Āryan races, but of Egypt, of North America and Mexico, of Arabia and Canaan, of China and Japan. Everywhere where philosophy—but this of course is comparatively seldom—has arisen in the midst of polytheists, it has perceived a unity behind the many, and has tended towards a more or less pantheistic Monotheism. Then, lastly—and this in only isolated cases—there has come a time when theological rivalries have lost their interest, and metaphysical discussions have lost their value; when men have tried, with more or less success, to seek for the summum bonum in various systems of self-culture in which the gods are practically disregarded, or quite left out of the account.

Comtism, Agnosticism and Buddhism are, it is true, the only systems which have broken away, in the most uncompromising manner, from the venerable soul-theories which have grown out of the ancient Animism. But Stoicism, Vedāntism, Confucianism and Deism, had come very near to the newer standpoint, and there is a whole side of Theism, and even of Christianity, which inculcates the same lesson. The kingdom of heaven that is within a man, the peace that passeth understanding, is the nearest analogue to the Buddhist Nirvāna which I know of in Western thought; and it is not the newer systems alone which insist upon the necessity of self-culture and of self-control.

It may be added that each of these various systems can also be said, in one sense, to have practically failed. Stoicism, Christianity, Comtism, Confucianism, Buddhism and all the rest, have so far disappointed the hopes of their founders, and of their early disciples. Though alike in many essential points, they differ one from another, not only in details, but in other things which their followers hold to be of the first importance. And the reason why they differ is the one thing in which they are most essentially alike. Each—though this will be admitted of Christianity only by those who think that the history of Christianity should be treated by the same methods as the history of other religions—each is the natural outcome of an immeasurable past, in which ideas, closely related no doubt, but always different, have undergone very slow and very gradual changes in directions similar, though in no case quite the same. Each has carried into its solution of the momentous problem it has had to face—and which each has faced with so great a degree of manfulness and earnestness—the inevitable influence of the long past it has inherited. Each, however widely it appealed to the people, however clear its repudiation of ranks and castes, however widely its doors stood open, has really been above the heads, beyond the grasp, of the general public of the nation among which it first appeared. And each, in putting new wine into the old bottles, in preserving many of the old phrases, has left a soil in which the old beliefs could again take root, and, nourished by the old ignorance and superstition, could grow up as a rank vegetation to counteract, if not to choke, all that was most beneficial and most true in the newer teaching.

We are deeply moved as we watch the representation by some powerful actor of the tragedy of the fall of some man or woman led on to destruction by the very conditions of their nature. How much greater the disaster when a whole nation, to whom the doors of liberty have once been opened, closes them upon itself, and relapses into the bondage of delusions! It would be hard to find, in the whole history of the world, a greater tragedy than that which was typified by the feast of

Jagan-nāth. The number of deaths at that festival has doubtless been sometimes exaggerated, and I am quite aware that reasons can be given for the hideous character of the carvings on the triumphal car of Vishṇu. But it is acknowledged that the temple at Purī had once been Buddhist, and that the very name Jagan-nāth—now supposed to be an actual spirit, a form of Vishnu—is really nothing but a misapplied ancient epithet, the Pāli Loka-nātha, of the great thinker and reformer of India. We know that deaths did, and up to very modern times, in fact take place, and were supposed to secure a happy entrance of the "soul" into realms of delight in heaven. When we call to mind how the frenzied multitudes, drunk with the luscious poison of delusions from which the reformation they had rejected might have saved them, dragged on that sacred car, heavy and hideous with carvings of obscenity and cruelty,—dragged it on in the name of Jagan-nāth, the forgotten teacher of enlightenment, of purity, and of universal love, while it creaked and crushed over the mangled bodies of miserable suicides, the victims of once exploded superstitions,—it will help us to realize how heavy is the hand of the immeasurable past; how much more powerful than the voice of the prophets is the influence of congenial fancies, and of inherited beliefs.

## LECTURE II.

# THE PĀLI PIṬAKAS.

---

THE belief of the orthodox Buddhists assigns the whole of the existing canonical books to the period immediately following the death of Gotama, and claims for them the sanction and authority, if not the authorship, of the immediate disciples of the Buddha himself.

It would be strange indeed if such a belief had not arisen. Many of the books purport to record the very words of the Master, or events in his life witnessed by his personal followers. There is no absolute statement in the books as to their date or authorship. Historical criticism was quite unknown in the early centuries of Buddhism, when men were concerned with matters they held to be vastly more important than exact statements of literary history. The tendency of the more devout minds among the early followers of Gotama would inevitably lead them to attach great importance to the books that had been handed down, and to assign to them therefore the highest possible antiquity. And when the idea that those very books had been in existence shortly after the death of the Buddha had once gained ground, any one who denied or even doubted the fact would be regarded with dislike, and avoided as a dangerous person.

But when impartial students, who are not orthodox Buddhists, come to read the Buddhist Scriptures in the light of the historical criticism which has grown up in modern times in Europe, and with historical rather than with religious objects in view, they perceive at once, from the internal evidence afforded by the books themselves, that the orthodox opinion can no longer be maintained. It is quite clear that the literature has been of gradual growth, and that, though the books as we now have them contain a great deal of older material, some of it perhaps reaching back to a time even before the death of Gotama, they cannot have been put into their present shape till long after that event.

When we attempt, however, to advance from this general proposition into more detailed statements, when we endeavour to form to ourselves any conception of the actual process by which the literature as a whole assumed its present form, we are beset by numerous difficulties. Those who have followed the course of speculation as to the origin and developement of the New Testament canon, or even only any one phase of it—such as the controversy raised by Strauss's work on the Life of Christ, the debate as to the authorship of the Gospel according to John, or the discussion between the author of "Supernatural Religion" and the Bishop of Durham—will easily understand how this is. The kind of questions that arise, the kind of arguments to which appeal has to be made, are much the same in the case of both literatures. And in both cases the final decision is apt to depend on personal impressions, whose validity is very much open to dispute.

It is true that Europeans come to the consideration of such questions, when they relate to the history of the Buddhist canon, with a degree of impartiality it would be unreasonable to expect, either from Christians or from Buddhists, when dealing with the literature of their own religion. There has therefore been much greater unanimity in such conclusions as have been already put forward by Pāli scholars. But, on the other hand, we know as yet much less about the Buddhist canon than we know about the Christian. The Buddhist Piṭakas, as their sacred books are collectively called, have not as yet been edited in anything like completeness. And we know much less, from other sources, of the history of the time in which they arose, than we know of the corresponding period in Christian history. The result is, at present, a degree of uncertainty even greater, if possible, in the one case than in the other. It will be noticed, however, that the reasons for this uncertainty are very different in the two cases. The materials on which the final decision as to the history of the New Testament will ultimately rest must be substantially the same as those which are now accessible. The present variety of opinion would seem, therefore, to be very greatly due to mental differences in the investigators themselves. In the case of the Pāli Piṭakas, the materials on which our judgment must rest are still for the most part hidden away in MSS.; and though these are now being published with encouraging rapidity, it would be unwise to occupy your time with conjectural discussions of questions which new evidence may any day decide for us one way or the other. I propose to confine myself, therefore, to a simple statement of those facts which are already known, and to an illustration, by one or two examples taken from the books themselves, of the character of the Pāli Suttas.

---

As is well known to you, the Buddha was not content merely to proclaim his new system to the world; he founded an Order, the members of which were to carry out the system and hand it down to future generations. There immediately arose a number of questions regarding the regulation of that Order, which are represented to have been settled in his lifetime by the Master himself—questions as to the admission to the Order; its internal government; its property; the relations of the members of the Order, male and female, to one another and to the outside world; the result of a breach by any member of the Rules of the Order, and so on.

The Order was a kind of republic. All proceedings were settled by resolutions agreed upon in regular meetings of its members, which were held subject to the observance of certain established regulations and to the use of certain fixed forms of words. The forms of words under which the meetings were conducted, and the resolutions passed, were called Kammavācās, that is, the "Words of the Act." They were naturally regarded with great reverence by the members of the Order, and they were handed down with scrupulous care. Though a large number of them have long ago fallen into abeyance, most, if not all, of them have survived down to the present day, and are extant in MSS. now existing in Buddhist countries, and sometimes to be found in our public libraries. There is good reason for the hope that our collections of these formularies—no doubt the most ancient forms recorded in the world's literature for preserving order and decorum in the conduct of general assemblies—will eventually be nearly, if not quite, complete. Only the other day, when a box of miscellaneous palm-leaf MSS. from different parts of India, now belonging to the Liverpool Free Library, was sent to me for report, I found among them a copy of several of these Kammavācās hitherto unknown to be still extant; and there are other MSS. of similar contents in the British Museum, and in the National Library at Paris, which have not yet been thoroughly examined.

The general outline of all these formularies is the same in all cases, and one example will suffice as a sample of all.

After a layman entered the Order, he often wished to choose a new name, or epithet, bearing some reference to his new aim of life—a custom which may well have arisen or received encouragement from the fact that the ordinary names in use "in the world" contained the name of a god, or otherwise implied an acknowledgment of the soul-theory which every member of the Order was supposed to have abandoned If a member desired thus to change his name, he would thrice state, formally, at a meeting of the Order, his desire to do so. Some learned and respected member would then on his behalf address the meeting thus:

"Let the venerable assembly hear me! Our Brother "A. B. requests permission to assume the name of "C. D. If the time is now meet for the assembly to "do so, the assembly will authorize our Brother A. B. "to assume the name C. D. Such is the proper course "in such a case.

"If any venerable member assent to permission "being granted to our Brother A. B. to assume the "name C. D., let him keep silence. If any venerable "member doth not assent, let him now speak."

Should no one speak on the opposite side, he would then continue:

"The assembly authorizes A. B. to assume the name "C. D. Therefore is the assembly silent. Thus do I "understand."

With these words, what we should call the motion (the ñatti) is considered to have been carried. The only amendment considered possible is apparently a direct negative; and there is no counting of votes, for no resolution is passed unless the meeting is unanimously in favour of it.

It will be noticed that no such officer as president or chairman is referred to. Whether there usually was one in ancient times we do not know; but in the few cases in which the use of these simple ceremonies—the only kind of ritual in use among orthodox Buddhists—still survives, it is the custom for the senior member present to preside over the meeting.

All the Kammavācās relate to the application of Rules already established to particular places, times or persons. They do not contemplate the discussion of any changes in the Rules themselves, nor of any points in doctrine, in discipline, or in the system of self-culture. We hear of such points being discussed in a conversational way in informal meetings, and even sometimes in actual assemblies of the Order, but the Kammavācās do not refer to them.

The Rules themselves, which were to be carried out, wherever possible, by such Kammavācās, are very few and simple. The object of joining the Order was supposed to be the attainment, in part or in whole, of the state of mental and moral culture called Arahatship. This was, of course, entirely a personal affair, and the matters to be settled by rule were only such as would naturally arise in a body of men following no worldly occupation, practically communists in respect of such property as the Order could possess, and holding no religious services and engaging in no prayers (in the Christian sense) of any kind at all.

Among the most important of the Rules are those concerning the holding of Uposatha, a regular meeting of the Order, the time of which was fixed, like the Sabbath, by the changes of the moon. At those meetings there was recited a work called the Pātimokkha, literally the "Disburdenment," a list of offences against ordinary morality, and against decorum in outward behaviour, by confession of which, guilty members of the Order could "disburden" themselves—that is, I think, in a double sense, both subjectively and in reference to their standing in the Order.

The other Rules deal exclusively with admission to the Order; the duties of seniors towards juniors, and vice versa; the yearly change of residence during the rainy season, and the holding of a ceremony called Pavāranā at its close; the use of various things deemed to be luxuries; the question of dress; the validity of formal resolutions of Order; the maintenance of discipline; the rules of hospitality; the conduct of the brethren and sisters to each other; and a few sanitary regulations and other miscellaneous points of minor importance.

Now one great division of the Buddhist Scriptures —the Vinaya Pitaka—is nothing else than what we should now call a text-book or manual of these various regulations and of the resolutions relating to them. And it is divided into three Parts: 1, the Khandakas, or "Chapters," containing the Rules; 2, the Sutta-vibhaŋga, or "Exposition of the Pātimokkha," containing a commentary on the so-called list of offences above mentioned; and 3, the Parivāra-pātha, or "Appendix," a sort of index and résumé of the other two.

The last of these three, the "Appendix," is, as you would naturally suppose, much later than the others, and, compared with them, of little independent value. The other two form an edition, evidently drawn up some considerable time after the formation of the Order, of the then existing regulations. In this edition, each separate regulation or offence is preceded by an introduction giving an account of the occasion on which the Buddha himself is said to have laid down or declared it; and is followed by what we should now call notes, setting forth exceptions, consequences, applications, and so on. Among these notes, I will mention in passing that we find the whole of an ancient commentary on the Pātimokkha, which must, of course, have been already in existence when the present "edition" was compiled.

No one is mentioned as the author of this edition of the Rules of the Buddhist Order; and indeed it probably had no author in our modern sense of that word. It is merely the last form reached by a literature which grew up in a gradual way. As to date, the great bulk of it must be older than the year 350 B.C. It received, however, its last touches about a century later; and it contains also some portions—such as the actual statement of the primary Rules, and of the various offences, and of the forms of the Kammavācās—which may even reach back to the lifetime of the Buddha himself. In other words, these books were in existence, practically as we now have them, within about 150 years after the time of Gotama; and they grew up out of older material, parts of which they have preserved intact. It will be seen below that a similar statement applies also to the rest of the books in the Pāli Pitakas. And amid the chaos which still reigns in the chronology of Indian literature it is a great gain to be able to fix the date of so important a literature within a so narrow limit of time.

This conclusion as to the age of the Vinaya Pitaka depends on a number of considerations which it would take a very considerable time—certainly the time allotted to the rest of this course of Lectures—to set out clearly and fully. The whole argument is much too intricate even to be summarized to advantage. And there are other matters, of greater interest from the point of view from which these Lectures are delivered, which demand our notice. I will only say, therefore, that the conclusions, as far as I have stated them, are accepted by all Pāli scholars; and that the details may be found in the Introduction to Dr. Oldenberg's edition of the whole text of the Vinaya Piṭaka (where the greater portion of the argument was first put forth), and in the Introduction to a complete translation of the Pātimokkha and of the Khandakas, which Dr. Oldenberg and myself are conjointly preparing for the series of translations from the Sacred Books of the East now being published at Oxford. These translations will consist of four volumes, of which the first, containing the Pātimokkha, is already published; the second is passing through the press; and the other two will appear at intervals of six months, so that the whole will be accessible to English readers before the close of next year.

---

The books which treat of the Buddhist Dhamma, that is to say, of its ethics and philosophy, and of its system of self-culture, will probably be considered by most to be of greater interest than those containing the regulations of the Order. They are divided, in a passage in one of the Khandakas just referred to, into five Nikāyas, or Collections, the whole of which have come down to us, though they exist as yet for the most part only in manuscript. It is the first four of these five Nikāyas (the Dīgha, Majjhima, Saŋyutta, and Aŋguttara Nikāyas) that contain the writings well known to you under the name of Suttas.

Of these Suttas, those in the first two Nikāyas contain the whole of the Dhamma considered in a series of long and short conversations, the principal interlocutor being usually Gotama himself, but occasionally Sāriputta, or some other of his principal disciples. And you will be able to judge of the style and tone of these conversations from the two examples of them which will be presently laid before you.

The Suttas, in the third Nikāya, give the same doctrines and in very much the same words, but in a different arrangement.

You will easily understand that it is often very difficult to gather from a series of dialogues the whole of the Buddha's teaching on any one point. As in the case of the Socratic Dialogues, to which these are in many respects very similar, opinions on the same or nearly allied points are found in many different Suttas; and the names of the dialogues, often merely proper names, are very little guide to their actual contents. To gather together, therefore, a complete statement of early Buddhist teaching on any question, it would be necessary to consult the whole of the dialogues in the first two Nikāyas, and to compare and combine the various utterances.

It is from this point of view that the Saŋyutta Nikāya—literally, "The Collection of Linked, or Arranged, Treatises"—has been made. In it all the paragraphs relating to any one subject are brought together, independently of the conversational form in which they are supposed to have been first delivered, and in which they appear in the two former Collections.

The question, then, naturally suggests itself, Which is the older form? Are the conversations built up out of the arranged treatises, or are these latter extracted from the conversations? To this question, no definite answer can as yet be given. We do not as yet know even whether the substance of the whole of the paragraphs in the third Nikāya will eventually be found in the first two; and it would be useless to debate probabilities on the scanty evidence at our command.

---

The fourth Nikāya, the Aŋguttara, contains once more very much the same matter, but again in a different order.

We have already had occasion incidentally to notice

how important is the place which numbers occupy in the statements of Buddhist truth. The "Noble Path" is eight-fold, and is divided into four stages, during which ten Saŋyojanas, or fetters, have to be broken. The wisdom to be attained by one walking in the path is of seven kinds; his spiritual powers, or senses, are five in number; and the struggle he has to carry on against his besetting weaknesses is divided into four aspects. In the same way, other parts of the Buddhist system are divided into classes of two, three, or more connected ideas.

But it must not be supposed that number played such a part in the early Buddhist philosophy as it played about the same time in the Pythagorean. These numbers are merely aids to memory, and have no mystical meaning. They should be compared rather with similar enumerations in early and mediæval Christianity, some of which are still familiar to us, such as the four gospels, the seven deadly sins, the eight cardinal virtues, the ten commandments, the twelve apostles, and so on.

It is with reference to this numerical statement of Buddhist ideas that the Aŋguttara Nikāya is arranged. All the classes containing only one thing are treated of in the first book, all the dyads in the second, all the triads in the third, and so on. And it may be said of this Nikāya, as of the last, that its contents, which often consist of the very words found in the conversational

Nikāyas, may either have been derived from them, or have existed before them.

---

None of these Four Great Collections, it will be seen, treats of only one subject. Each of them contains practically the whole of the Buddhist teaching. It is unlikely that any one point is exclusively treated by any one of them. And they are all divided into Suttas, each conversation of the first two being called a Sutta (or a Suttanta, as the older phraseology had it), and each different statement in the two latter being also called a Sutta, though these last Suttas are of course much shorter than the others.

The last of the Nikāyas, on the other hand, consists of fifteen miscellaneous books of poetry, legends, &c., very much more like our modern books, and, for that very reason, probably later than the Great Collections of the Suttas. There was from very early times a difference of opinion among orthodox Buddhists as to the exact number of books which ought to be included in this division—a difference of opinion which would scarcely have been possible had all the books contained in it been as old as the Vinaya and the Suttas. Probably the number of writings in this miscellaneous collection was varied from time to time, chiefly by additions made to it.

---

At a period not yet determined, but probably some centuries after the death of Gotama, there came into use another division of the whole literature into three Pitakas, literally "Baskets," meaning, I think, Bodies of Tradition.[1] The first of these three was the Vinaya Pitaka, as above described; the second was the Sutta Piṭaka, consisting of the four great collections of the Suttas; and the third, containing the books of the fifth Nikāya and seven other prose works, was called collectively the Abhidhamma Piṭaka.

There has been much misconception as to this third name. It has been explained as meaning metaphysics; but so far as anything is as yet known of the Abhidhamma books, they are by no means more metaphysical than the other parts of the Pitakas. There is indeed but very little metaphysics in early Buddhism, and "Abhidhamma" would seem to bear much more the relation to "Dhamma" which "by-law" bears to "law," than that which "metaphysics" bears to "physics." The so-called Dīgha-bhānakā, that is, those

[1] Mr Trenckner suggests, in his Pāli Miscellany, p 68, that baskets may have been used, when wheelbarrows were unknown, in excavating ground, and may have been passed from hand to hand, as fire-buckets now are And he quotes two interesting passages from the Majjhima Nikāya, in which the Brāhman are ridiculed as handing down their doctrines "basket-wise" (piṭaka-sampadāya) But the earliest use of the word by Buddhists when speaking of their own books is very much later than the canonical books themselves See, further, Appendix VIII.

members of the Order whose duty it was to repeat and hand down the Dīgha Nikāya, included in the Abhidhamma Piṭaka even the books of lighter literature, poetry, legends, and the like, which form the fifth Nikāya. Could they have done so if the word Abhidhamma had conveyed to the early Buddhists exclusively the idea of what we now call metaphysics?

This use of the term Abhidhamma Piṭaka has the advantage of confining the term Sutta Pitaka to those four Collections which do actually consist of Suttas. But another ancient school, that of the repeaters of the Majjhima Nikāya, include the fifth Nikāya with the four others in the Sutta Piṭaka, and confine the term Abhidhamma Piṭaka to the seven prose works, supplementary to the Suttas, above referred to. These, like the fifteen books of the fifth Nikāya, are probably each the work of a single author, and are to be distinguished from the fifteen chiefly by the fact that they deal rather with questions of doctrine than with poetry or legend. All these twenty-two works, forming the Abhidhamma Piṭaka, were probably in existence before the end of the third century before the Christian era. The four great collections of the Suttas were no doubt much older, and the more important of them were as old, if not older, than the date assigned above to the Vinaya Pitaka. I must refer you for a detailed discussion of this question to the Introduction to my translation of the longest of these older Suttas, the Mahā-parinibbāna Sutta, in Vol. XI. of the Sacred Books of the East, and invite your attention now to the actual contents of these ancient writings.

---

The method of composition employed in the older Suttas will best be understood by the examples above referred to. Let us take, as a first instance, the

### ASSALĀYANA SUTTA
OF THE
### MAJJHIMA NIKĀYA.[1]

It opens by describing how a number of Brāhmans at Sāvatthi were trying to find some one who could controvert the opinion put forward by Gotama, that all the four castes were equally pure. In their difficulty they apply to a young and distinguished scholar, named Assalāyana, whom they think equal to the contest. He objects that Gotama is a dhamma-vādī, one who reasons according to the truth (not, that is, on the basis of the authority of the Vedas, or of tradition), and that those who reason thus are difficult to overcome. However, after repeated solicitation, he reluctantly consents to their request, goes to the place

---

[1] It has been edited by Professor Pischel of Kiel (Chemnitz, 1880), with an English version. It is not the third Sutta of the Nikāya, as he states in his preface, but the third Sutta in the Brāhmana Vagga, that is, the ninety-third in the Nikāya.

where Gotama was staying, and after exchanging with him greetings of civility and courtesy, takes a seat by his side. Then he asks:

"The Brāhmans, O Gotama, say thus: 'The Brāh-
"'mans are the best caste (literally, the best colour):
"'every other caste is inferior. The Brāhmans are
"'the white caste: every other caste is black. The
"'Brāhmans alone are pure: those who are not Brāh-
"'mans are not pure. The Brāhmans are the (only)
"'real sons of Brahmā, born from his mouth, sprung
"'from Brahmā, created by Brahmā, heirs of Brahmā.'
"But what do you, Sir, say about this?"

Then the Buddha asks him whether the wives of the Brāhmans are not subject to all the ills and disabilities of child-birth to which other women are subject.

Assalāyana is obliged to confess that this is so, and that the Brāhmans put forward their claims in spite of this.

The Buddha then, applying our modern comparative method of inquiry, asks whether in adjacent countries, such as Bactria and Afghanistan, there are not differences of colour similar to those between the Brāhmans and other castes, and yet in those countries whether slaves cannot become masters, and masters become slaves.

Again Assalāyana confesses the fact, and that the Brāhmans put forward their claims in spite of it.

Then Gotama goes on to ask: "How think you, Assa-

"lāyana—a man who is a murderer, a thief, a libertine, "a liar, a slanderer, violent or frivolous in speech, "covetous, malevolent, given to false doctrine—will "such an one, if he be a Khattiya, or a Vessa, or a "Sudda, be born after death, when the body is dis-"solved into some unhappy state of misery and woe, "but not if he be a Brāhman?"

Assalāyana replies that the Brāhman is in this respect exactly on a par with the others

Gotama then proceeds to put the contrary case, when Assalāyana declares that those who do the contrary of all these evil things are equally re-born into some happy state in heaven, whether they are Brāhmans or whether they are not.

Gotama asks what force or what comfort there can then be in the claim to especial purity which the Brāhmans make. But he carries the argument still further. "What think you, Assalāyana, is it the Brāhman "alone who is able, in this land of ours, to cultivate "friendliness, kindliness, charitable feelings; or can "the Khattiya, the Vessa and the Sudda do so too?"

And when Assalāyana acknowledges that they are all equal in this respect, Gotama compels him to grant also that they are equally pure in their bodies, and that the flame kindled by an outcast by means of two pieces of wood belonging to a dog's drinking vessel or a pig-sty, will light a sacred fire as shining and beaming and bright, and as good for sacrificial purposes, as a flame kindled by a Brāhman or a Khattiya by means of sweet-smelling sandal-wood!

Then, still questioning, Gotama points out how—whereas when a mare is united with an ass, the offspring is a mule, different from both father and mother—the union of a Khattiya and a Brāhman, or vice versâ, results in offspring which resembles both the parents, with the obvious suggestion that there is not really any difference of species or caste between Khattiya or Brāhman and half-caste or low-caste men, as there is in the case of a donkey and a horse.

Finally, Gotama asks the young Brāhman scholar, "to which of two brothers, one an initiated student "and the other not, the Brāhmans themselves would, "on sacred and solemn occasions, give the precedence?"

"To the initiated student," says Assalāyana; "for "what thing given to an uninitiated person, not a "student, will bear with it great advantage?"

"But if the initiated student be of bad character "and evil habits, and the other be of good character "and virtuous habits," rejoins Gotama, "to whom then "will the Brāhmans themselves give the precedence?"

"To the uninitiated," is the reply; "for what thing "given to a man of bad character and of evil habits "will bring with it great advantage?"

"But in the former answer you yourself, Assa-"lāyana," says the Master, "have given up the pre-"eminence of birth, and in the latter the pre-eminence "of acquaintance with the sacred words. And in doing "so you yourself have acknowledged that purity of "all the castes which I proclaim!"

"When he had thus spoken, the young Brāhman "Assalāyana," says the Sutta, "sat there silent, awk-"ward, distressed, looking downwards, reflecting, not "able to answer!"

Then Gotama tells a story, winding up with a kind word to the young scholar. And the Sutta concludes with the confession of Assalāyana: "Most excellent, "Gotama, are the words of thy mouth—most excellent! "May the venerable Gotama receive me as a disciple "and as a true believer, from this day forth as long as "life endures!"

---

It will be seen that this Sutta is merely of a negative character, the interlocutor being defeated, as it were, out of his own mouth by a kind of argumentum ad hominem, in which nothing is assumed but that which the opponent himself will grant.

Let us therefore take another Sutta, in which the positive side of Gotama's teaching comes into view, though only the lower morality of the unconverted man, the Ādi-brahma-cariyaŋ, not the higher system of the Noble Path, the Magga-brahma-cariyaŋ. As in the Sutta we have just summarized, nothing is assumed in the argumentative part of this one which the opposite side do not themselves acknowledge. As in the last example, time will not allow me to give more than an abstract, but a complete version can be found in the volume of translations already referred to.[1] I have there rendered the title, "On "Knowledge of the Vedas;" the Pāli name is,

THE TEVIJJA SUTTA
OF THE
DĪGHA NIKĀYA.

A number of wealthy and distinguished Brāhmans are represented as staying at a pleasant spot called Manasākaṭa, on the banks of the Rapti. There they had built themselves huts in a fenced enclosure, where they were in the habit of meeting together to repeat their mantras, the wonder-working sacred words of the Vedas.

Two young Brāhmans, Vāseṭṭha and Bhāradvāja, after learning by heart and repeating all day, go down in the evening to the river-side to bathe, and then walk up and down on the sandy beach.

"Now a conversation sprang up between Vāseṭṭha "and Bhāradvāja, when they were thus taking exer-"cise after their bath, and walking up and down in "thoughtful mood, as to which was the true path, and "which the false."

---

[1] Buddhist Suttas from the Pāli, pp. 156—203.

Each of them adduces the authority of a Brāhman teacher, learned in the Scriptures; and when neither is able to convince the other, Vāseṭṭha says, "That "Samana Gotama, Bhāradvāja, of the Sakya clan, who "left the Sakya tribe to adopt the religious life, is now "staying at Manasākaṭa, in the mango-grove on the "bank of the river to the south of Manasākaṭa. Now "regarding that venerable Gotama, such is the high "reputation that has been noised abroad, that he is said "to be 'a fully enlightened one, blessed and worthy, "'abounding in wisdom and goodness, happy, with "'knowledge of the worlds, a blessed Buddha.' Come "then, Bhāradvāja, let us go to the place where the "Samana Gotama is; and having done so, let us ask "the Samana Gotama touching this matter. What "the Samana Gotama shall declare unto us, that let us "bear in mind!"

So they go to the Master and lay their difficulty before him, Vāseṭṭha being the spokesman. When Gotama hears that they both depend upon authority, he wants to know what is the dispute, the difference of opinion between them.

"Just, Gotama, as near a village or a town there are "many and various paths, yet they all meet together "in the village; just in that way are all the various "paths taught by various Brāhmans—the Addhariya "Brāhmans, the Tittiriya Brāhmans, the Chandoka "Brāhmans, the Chandava Brāhmans, the Brahma-

"cariya Brāhmans—are all these saving paths? Are "they all paths which will lead him who acts according "to them into a state of union with Brahmā?

"Do you say that they all lead aright, Vāseṭṭha?"

"I say so, Gotama."

"Do you really say that they all lead aright, Vāseṭ-"ṭha?"

"So I say, Gotama."

"But then, Vāseṭṭha, is there a single one of the "Brāhmans versed in the three Vedas, or of their "pupils, or of their teachers, or of their forerunners up "to the seventh generation, who has ever seen Brahmā "face to face?"

To each of these questions, Vāseṭṭha answers "No."

"Well, then, Vāseṭṭha, those ancient Rishis of the "Brāhmans, versed in the three Vedas, the authors of "the verses, the utterers of the verses, whose ancient "form of words so chanted, uttered or composed, the "Brāhmans of to-day chant over again or repeat, in-"toning or reciting exactly as has been intoned or "recited—did even they speak thus, saying, 'We "'know it, we have seen it, where Brahmā is, whence "'Brahmā is, whither Brahmā is?'"

"Not so, Gotama."

"Then you say, Vāseṭṭha, that not one of the Brāh-"mans, even up to the seventh generation, has ever "seen Brahmā face to face. And that even the Rishis "of old, the authors and utterers of those ancient words "which the Brāhmans of to-day so carefully intone and "recite, precisely as they have been handed down— "even they did not pretend to know, or to have seen, "where or whence or whither Brahmā is. So that the "Brāhmans, versed in the three Vedas, have forsooth "said this: 'What we know not, neither have seen, "'to a state of union with that can we show the way!' "Just, Vāsettha, as, when a string of blind men are "clinging one to the other, neither can the foremost "see, nor can the middle one see, nor can the hinder-"most see—just even so, methinks, Vāseṭṭha, is the "talk of the Brāhmans, versed though they be in the "three Vedas, but blind talk. The first sees not, "neither does his teacher see, nor does his pupil. The "talk, then, of these Brāhmans, versed in their three "Vedas, turns out to be ridiculous, mere words, a vain "and empty thing!"

This result is here concisely stated, though in the words of the original it has not been reached without further questions. In a similar way, Vāseṭṭha acknowledges that the Brāhmans cannot show the way to a state of union with the sun and the moon gods whom they can see: on which follows an obvious rejoinder very much as above, concluding with:

"Just, Vāseṭṭha, as if a man should say, 'How I "'long for, how I love, the most beautiful woman in "'this land!'

"And people should ask him, 'Well, good friend!

"'this most beautiful woman in the land, whom you
"'thus love and long for, do you know whether that
"'beautiful woman is a noble lady, or a Brāhman
"'woman, or of the trader class, or a Sudda?'

"And when so asked, he should answer, 'No!'

"And when people should ask him, 'Well, good
"'friend! this most beautiful woman in all the land,
"'whom you so love and long for, do you know what
"'her name is, or her family name; whether she be
"'tall or short, dark or of medium complexion, black
"'or fair; or in what village or town or city she
"'dwells?'

"But when so asked, he should answer, 'No!'

"And then people should say to him, 'So then, good
"'friend! whom you know not, neither have seen, her
"'do you love and long for?'

"And then, when so asked, he should answer, 'No!'

"Now what think you, Vāseṭṭha? Would it not
"turn out, that being so, that the talk of that man
"was foolish talk?"

"In sooth, Gotama, it would," replies Vāsettha, though he knows now what will be the rejoinder to follow. After another simile, or parable, very forcible in its way, which I must omit, Gotama continues:

"Again, Vāseṭṭha, if this great river Rapti were
"full of water, even to the brim, and overflowing, and
"a man with business for the other side, bound for
"the other side, should come up and want to cross

"over, and he, standing on this bank, were to invoke "the further bank, and say, 'Come hither, further "'bank! come over to this side!' Now what think "you, Vāseṭṭha? Would the further bank of the "Rapti, by means of that man's invoking, and praying, "and hoping, and praising, come over to this side?"

"Certainly not, Gotama!"

"In just the same way, Vāseṭṭha, do the Brāhmans, "versed in the three Vedas—but omitting the prac-"tice of those *qualities* which really make a man a "Brāhman, and adhering to those things which really "make men not Brāhmans—say thus: 'Indra we call "'upon: Soma we call upon: Varuna we call upon: "'Isāna we call upon: Pajāpati we call upon: Brahmā "'we call upon: Mahiddhi we call upon: Yama we "'call upon!' Verily, Vāseṭṭha, that these Brāhmans "—so long as they omit the practice of virtue, and "follow after evil—that they, by reason of their "invoking, and praying, and hoping, and praising, "should, after death, and when the body is dissolved, "become united with Brahmā—verily, such a condi-"tion of things has no existence!"

Then, by other similes and other questions, each as elaborately worked out, Gotama shows how yielding to one's senses and one's lusts, how malice, sloth, pride, self-righteousness and doubt, must in fact be bonds and hindrances and entanglements, which, from Vāsettha's own point of view, will prevent any real union with

God. And he concludes his last point, and with it the negative side of his argument, thus:

"Then you say, Vāseṭṭha, that the Brāhmans are "in possession of wives and wealth, and that Brahmā "is not. Can there then be agreement and likeness "between the Brāhmans, with their wives and pro- "perty, and Brahmā, who has none of these things?"

"Certainly not, Gotama!"

"And you say too, Vāseṭṭha, that the Brāhmans "bear anger and malice in their hearts, and are sinful "and uncontrolled, whilst Brahmā is free from anger "and malice, and is sinless, and has self-mastery. "Now can there then be concord and likeness between "the Brāhmans and Brahmā?"

"Certainly not, Gotama!"

"Very well then, Vāseṭṭha! That these Brāh- "mans, versed though they be in their three Vedas, "and yet bearing anger and malice in their hearts, "sinful and uncontrolled, should, after death and "when the body is dissolved, become united to Brahmā, "who is just the opposite of all this—such a condition "of things has no existence!

"So that thus, then, Vāseṭṭha, the Brāhmans, while "they sit down in confidence in their knowledge of "the Vedas, are really sinking down in mire. And "so sinking, they are arriving only at despair, think- "ing the while that they are crossing over into some "happier land! Therefore is it that the three-fold "wisdom of the Brāhmans, wise in the Vedas, is called "a waterless desert, their three-fold wisdom is called "a pathless jungle, their three-fold wisdom is called "destruction!"

Vāseṭṭha, deeply moved, asks the Master whether he can show the way to union with Brahmā, and, when he hears that he can, humbly beseeches him to do so, closing his appeal with the words, "Let the venerable Gotama save the Brāhman race."

Then the Master sets forth his scheme of elementary morality, which, as was called attention to above, is below and introductory to the higher morality of the Noble Path. With a great deal of it we cannot agree, but it is not the less historically interesting on that account. As he is addressing Vāseṭṭha and Bhāradvāja, he first lays stress upon the advantages of joining his Order; but this was not considered in early Buddhism to be necessary, though it was held to be conducive, to the practice of either the lower morality here described, or the more advanced condition of those who have entered the Path. What we are now to hear is not a complete statement of the Buddha's own view of life—that would be a description of Arahatship—but the Buddha's answer to the particular question propounded to him, namely, What is the right way to a state of union with Brahmā? Gotama begins:

"Know, Vasettha, that from time to time a Tathāgata "is born into the world, a fully Enlightened One, "blessed and worthy, abounding in wisdom and goodness, happy, with knowledge of the world, unsurpassed as a guide to erring mortals, a teacher of gods and men, a Blessed Buddha. He, by himself, thoroughly understands, and sees, as it were, face to face this universe—the world below with all its spirits, and the worlds above, of Māra and of Brahmā—and all creatures, Samanas and Brāhmans, gods and men, and he then makes his knowledge known to others. The truth doth he proclaim both in its letter and in its spirit, lovely in its origin, lovely in its progress, lovely in its consummation: the higher life doth he make known, in all its purity and in all its perfectness.

"A householder (gahapati), or one of his children, or a man of inferior birth in any class, listens to that truth.[1] On hearing the truth he has faith in the Tathāgata, and when he has acquired that faith he thus considers with himself:

"'Full of hindrances is household life, a path defiled by passion: free as the air is the life of him who has renounced all worldly things. How difficult is it for the man who dwells at home to live the higher life in all its fulness, in all its purity, in all its bright perfection! Let me then cut off my hair and

[1] The point is, that the acceptance of this "Doctrine and Discipline" is open to all, not of course that Brāhmans never accept it.

"'beard, let me clothe myself in the orange-coloured "'robes, and let me go forth from a household life into "'the homeless state!'

"Then before long, forsaking his portion of wealth, "be it great or be it small; forsaking his circle of "relatives, be they many or be they few, he cuts off "his hair and beard, he clothes himself in the orange-"coloured robes, and he goes forth from the household "life into the homeless state.

"When he has thus become a recluse, he passes a "life self-restrained according to the rules of the "Pātimokkha; uprightness is his delight, and he sees "danger in the least of those things he should avoid; "he adopts and trains himself in the precepts; he "encompasses himself with holiness in word and deed; "he sustains his life by means that are quite pure; "good is his conduct, guarded the door of his senses; "mindful and self-possessed, he is altogether happy!"[1]

---

[1] The argument is resumed after the Three Sīlas, or Descriptions of Conduct—a text, doubtless older than the Suttas in which it occurs, setting forth the distinguishing moral characteristics of a member of the Order.

The First Sīla is an expansion of the Ten Precepts ("Buddhism," p. 160), but omitting the fifth, against the use of intoxicating drinks. The Second Sīla is a further expansion of the first and then of the last four, and finally of the fourth Precept. The Third Sīla is directed against auguries, divinations, prophecies, astrology, quackery, ritualism, and the worship of gods (including Brahmā).

These Three Sīlas may perhaps have been inserted in the Sutta

"Now wherein, Vāseṭṭha, is his conduct good?

"Herein, O Vāseṭṭha, that putting away the murder "of that which lives, he abstains from destroying life. "The cudgel and the sword he lays aside; and, full of "modesty and pity, he is compassionate and kind to "all creatures that have life!

"This is the kind of goodness that he has.

"Putting away the theft of that which is not his, "he abstains from taking anything not given. He "takes only what is given, therewith is he content, and "he passes his life in honesty and in purity of heart!

"This, too, is the kind of goodness that he has.

"Putting away unchastity, he lives a life of chastity "and purity, averse to the low habit of sexual inter-"course.

"This, too, is the kind of goodness that he has.

"Putting away lying, he abstains from speaking "falsehood. He speaks truth, from the truth he never "swerves; faithful and trustworthy, he injures not his "fellow-man by deceit.

"This, too, is the kind of goodness that he has.

"Putting away slander, he abstains from calumny. "What he hears here he repeats not elsewhere to raise "a quarrel against the people here: what he hears

---

as a kind of counterpoise to the Three Vedas Our Sutta really reads better without them, but they are interesting in themselves, and the third is especially valuable as evidence of ancient customs and beliefs "elsewhere he repeats not here to raise a quarrel "against the people there. Thus he lives as a binder "together of those who are divided, an encourager of "those who are friends, a peacemaker, a lover of peace, "impassioned for peace, a speaker of words that make "for peace.

"This, too, is the kind of goodness that he has.

"Putting away bitterness of speech, he abstains "from harsh language. Whatever word is humane, "pleasant to the ear, lovely, reaching to the heart, "urbane, pleasing to the people, beloved of the people "—such are the words he speaks.

"This, too, is the kind of goodness that he has.

"Putting away foolish talk, he abstains from vain "conversation. In season he speaks; he speaks that "which is; he speaks fact; he utters good doctrine; he "utters good discipline; he speaks, and at the right "time, that which redounds to profit, is well-grounded, "is well-defined, and is full of wisdom.

"This, too, is the kind of goodness that he has"

Other paragraphs follow, first shorter and then longer, which concern only members of the Order, and not laymen. Then a series of still longer paragraphs, dissuading from the practice of all the various customs and ceremonies dependent upon the Animism then, and unfortunately long afterwards, current in India. We find in these lists all kinds of auguries, divinations, interpretations of omens, marks on the body, and dreams; offerings, sacrifices, spells, prophecies, astrology; casuistry, vows, rituals and ceremonies, only mentioned to be condemned as worse than useless. And Gotama then addresses himself to the positive side of his argument, to the enumeration of the practices that he puts in place of these Animistic follies.

"And he lets his mind pervade one quarter of the "world with thoughts of Love; and so the second, "and so the third, and so the fourth. And thus the "whole wide world, above, below, around, and every-"where, does he continue to pervade with heart "of Love, far-reaching, grown great and beyond "measure!"

This paragraph is then repeated, substituting for Love, in the first paragraph Pity, in the second Sympathy, in the third Evenness of Mind. And to each of these there is a simile and a conclusion, thus:

"Just, Vāsettha, as a mighty trumpeter makes him-"self heard—and that without difficulty—in all the "four directions, even so of all things that have shape "or life, there is not one that he passes by or leaves "aside, but regards them all with mind set free and "deep-felt love!

"Verily, this, Vāseṭṭha, is the way to a state of "union with Brahmā!"

Finally, after comparing the condition of heart of the man who acts up to all these things with the character which Vāsettha acknowledges that the Brāh-

*Toran or East Gatewdy of the Stupa of Barhut, Restored from Fragments. About 185-72 B.C.*

*Woman with plain Hair Bun, Cave XVI, Right wall, Ajanta c. 500—510 A.D.*

*"A Divinity worshipping the Buddha", Cave XVI; Verandah, Left wall, Ajanta c. 600 A.D.*

*"Crowned Male Personage", Left wall, Cave XVII, Ajanta c. 650 A.D.*

*Votive Stupa from Monastery 12: Nalanda*

*Relief showing eight scenes from Buddha's life: Nalanda*

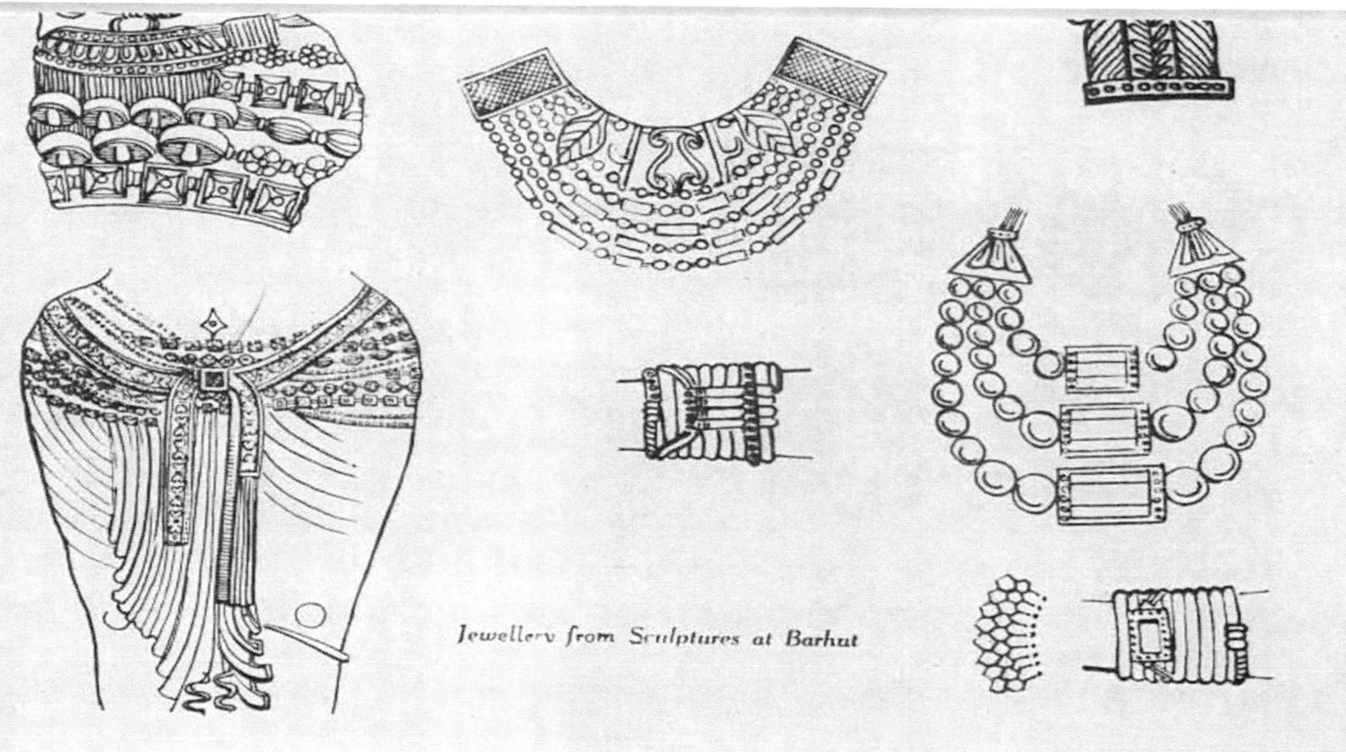

*Jewellery from Sculptures at Barhut*

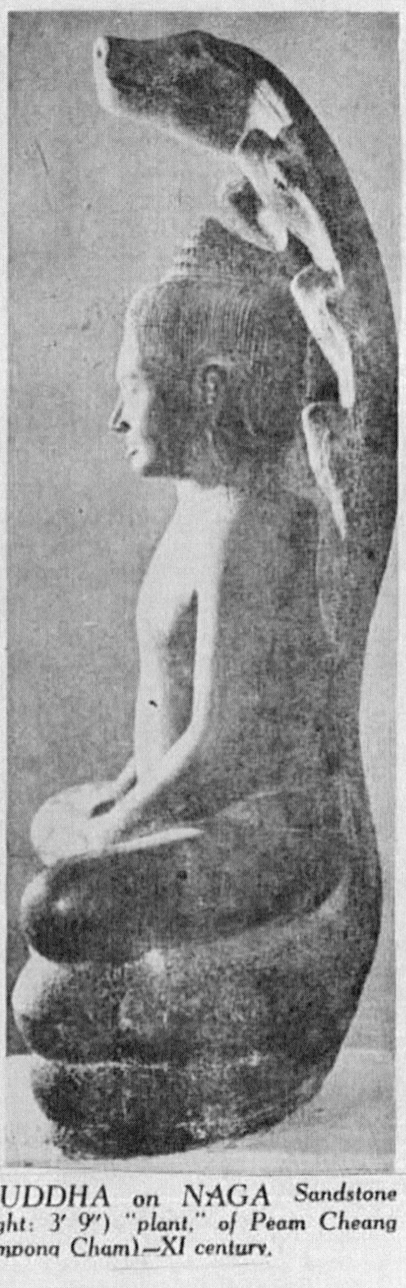

BUDDHA on NAGA Sandstone (height: 3′ 9″) "plant." of Peam Cheang (Kompong Cham)—XI century.

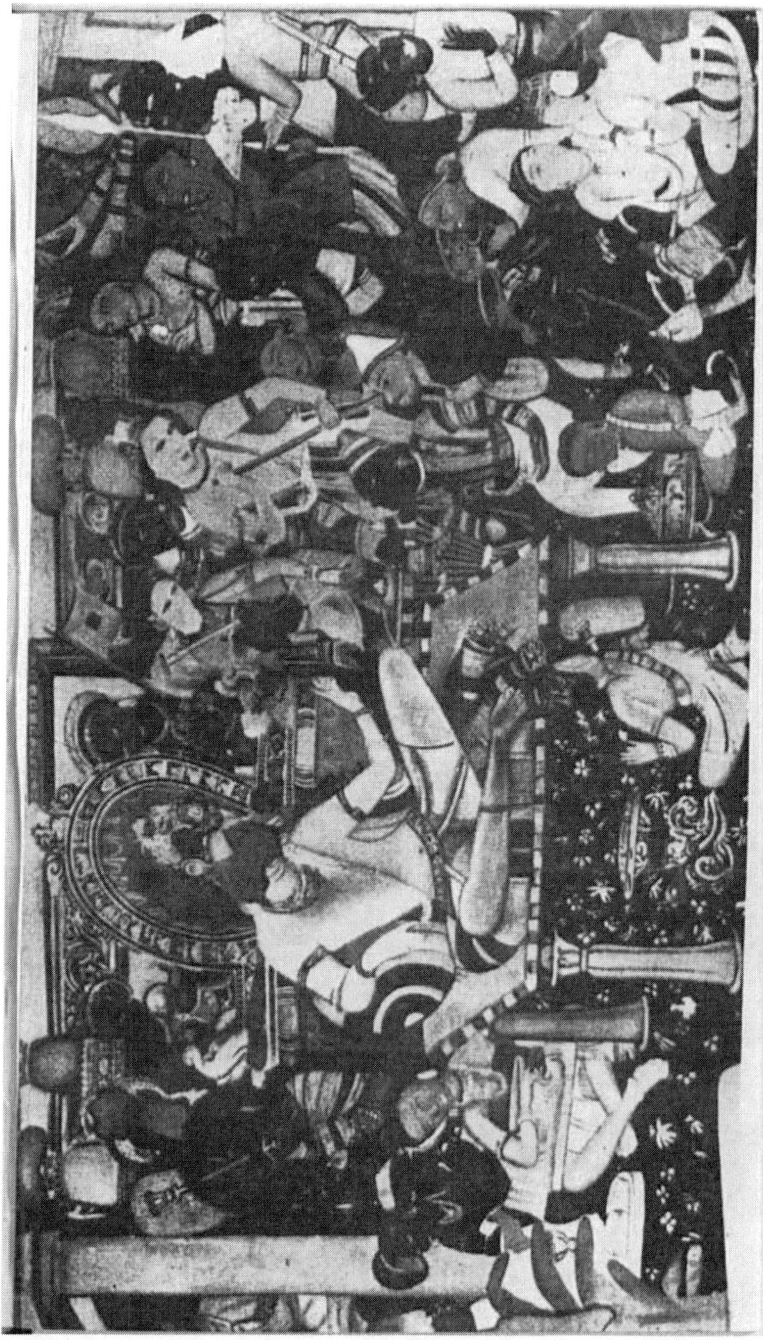

*Jaggayyapeta: The Stupa Panel. The Universal King. 1st Century B. C.*

mans themselves ascribe to Brahmā, the conclusion is reached:

"Then in sooth, Vāsettha, that such a man—who is "kind, and full of love, and pure in mind, and master "of himself—that he, after death and when the body "is dissolved, should become united with Brahmā, "such a condition of things is every way possible!"

After this, we cannot be surprised that the Sutta again, as in the former case, closes with the statement that "Vāsettha and Bhāradvāja addressed the Blessed "One, and said:

"Most excellent, Lord, are the words of thy mouth, "most excellent! Just as if a man were to set up "that which is thrown down, or were to reveal that "which is hidden away, or were to point out the right "road to him who has gone astray, or were to bring "a lamp into the darkness, so that those who have "eyes can see external forms;—just even so, Lord, "has the truth been made known to us, in many a "figure, by the Blessed One. And we, even we, "betake ourselves, Lord, to the Blessed One as our "refuge, to the Truth, and to the Brotherhood. "May the Blessed One accept us as disciples, as "true believers, from this day forth, as long as life "endures!"

I will only add, to avoid a very natural misconception, that such a union with Brahmā as is here referred to, is not supposed, in early Buddhism, to be the highest thing which men should seek after. According to the theory of Karma, which will be explained in the next Lecture, it would only be a new being, who has no conscious personal identity with the man who has lived such a life, who would thus achieve a merely temporary union with a merely temporary Brahmā. There can be no finality in such a union; it must end, like every other life, save that of the Arahat, in rebirth. And far better than that, an aim far worthier of the truly intelligent man, is to reach here on earth the Nirvāna of a perfect life in Arahatship, which, it is true, includes all that we have heard of just now, but which also includes much more.

---

I will now only detain you—and I must thank you for listening with so much attention to what has been a necessary, though I am afraid a somewhat tedious, sketch of the early Buddhist literature—while I make an announcement which I am sure you will hear with pleasure. As was said in the course of the Lecture, the Vinaya Pitaka, the Collection of the Rules of the Order, is already in the course of publication, and the more important parts of it are being translated into English. But the Suttas, which seem to me to be in many respects far more valuable and interesting, still lie buried and unpublished in Pāli MSS., which few people can read and fewer still can understand. There has for some time been a correspondence going on between the leading Pāli scholars in Europe, and they have all received with a welcome, not short of enthusiastic, a proposal to form a Society for the publication of the original texts of the whole of these curious and ancient books. The scholars referred to are willing to give their services gratuitously, and I trust before long we shall have both texts and translations into English of all the Suttas, and of the supplementary Abhidhamma books, available for the use of those who wish to find out what early Buddhism really was. All that is wanted is, that a few of those who have the money should join with those who have the necessary knowledge, by subscribing towards the cost of printing. I am empowered, therefore, by the Committee of the Pāli Text Society, as the young Society will be called, to inform you to-day of its birth. Two hundred subscribers of a guinea a-year will make it a success. The scholars who will do the work without pecuniary reward of any kind, have already promised to subscribe themselves, and a few donations of larger sums would make the matter comparatively easy. I need say nothing on the importance of such an undertaking, especially with reference to a right understanding of the oiigin and growth of religious belief. Your presence here to-day sufficiently proves your sympathy with such an object. I will only conclude, therefore, with an earnest appeal to those who can help in this matter, to give their cordial and practical co-operation to a cause so good, that all who are fortunate enough to be fellow-workers in it will feel a just pride when it has been carried by their aid to a successful accomplishment.[1]

---

[1] I have thought it right, after some hesitation, to retain these last sentences as they originally stood. A few hundred pounds are still required to make up the necessary amount, and in a wealthy country like England, where thousands are constantly being raised for objects not more deserving, I trust that the deficiency will, before long, be entirely supplied by those who sympathize with the proposed undertaking. A fuller statement of the present state of the Society will be found at the end of the volume, and any one who is willing to help can there see what is still required.

LECTURE III

# THE BUDDHIST THEORY OF KARMA.

---

In the first Lecture we endeavoured to estimate the general position of Buddhism in the religious history, firstly of India, and secondly of the world at large. In the closing sentences stress was laid upon the fact that Buddhism was in a great degree the pouring of new wine into old bottles, and the disastrous effect of its method in this respect was touched upon. In no particular was this more the case than in its teaching about the belief, then an unquestioned and universal belief in India, of the transmigration of souls.

This doctrine, as has been already pointed out, is entirely absent from the Vedas; and the question naturally arises, Where did it come from? Anthropologists seem to be of the opinion that it was world-wide in its distribution, and that it may be found everywhere in the lower stages of civilization. But they must admit that there is not the least evidence to show that the Āryans, before their dispersion, had passed through this stage of belief; and I venture to doubt whether the doctrine of the transmigration of souls has ever been independently arrived at or generally held among any one of the seven races into which the Āryans were subsequently distributed. This suggestion has, I am afraid, the disadvantage of novelty; but the importance of the fact, if it turn out to be true, will, I trust, justify the desire at least to raise a question the decision of which I must leave to abler hands. If the Āryan races cannot be shown to have entertained a belief otherwise so widely spread, it shows how great should be the caution with which we can venture to argue from the beliefs of one race to those of another; and it also offers a fresh confirmation of the fact that the course of early religious belief is by no means everywhere quite the same. The general term Animism is, indeed, a convenient expression for a rudimentary philosophy, which seems to have been almost, if not quite, universal. But races who have not as yet advanced beyond it, who see spirits everywhere, and find in the action of spirits a natural explanation of every mysterious event, are not likely to be capable of simultaneously entertaining very many ideas, or of carrying out any general principle to its logical conclusions. Of the various delusions that result from this Animistic conception of things, each individual, each tribe, has held only a few; the details themselves are necessarily, therefore, different; some are more persistent than others, and none are universal.

Mr. Tylor, in his "Primitive Culture," which always seems to me one of the most interesting books that our language contains, has carefully collected evidence regarding various curious notions allied to the Indian belief in the transmigration of souls.[1] But among the many instances he has adduced, there is not one which shows the idea among any Āryan people uninfluenced from outside. Indeed, the only instances he gives which are Āryan at all, are the well-known cases of Pythagoras and Plato; and while neither of these writers held the Indian notion, either in its Hindū or in its Buddhist form, neither of them have preserved to us, in the views they did hold, a product of the native mind of the Greeks. Their views of the continued existence after death of the human soul in the bodies of other men, or of beasts, are philosophical speculations of isolated thinkers acquainted with foreign modes of thought, not the universally accepted beliefs of ordinary people. They are most probably modifications of Egyptian ideas (such as those referred to by Herodotus, ii. 123), which are themselves very different from the Indian belief.

---

[1] Vol. ii pp 1—10.

Mr. Tylor might have mentioned Empedocles, who is reported to have said that he had been "a boy, a "girl, a bush, a bird, a fish."[1] Or he might have quoted Cæsar's report of a supposed tenet of the Druids that "souls do not die, but pass at death from one to another; and that this was a great incentive to virtue, for the fear of death was disregarded."[2] And my father has pointed out to me a curious Irish legend, recorded in the so-called Book of Balimote, which certainly savours strongly of transmigration. As this work is not easily accessible, I will quote the passage. The poet is excusing himself for beginning his history a thousand years before his hero was born. It seems that his hero was really alive all the while.

"1. Tuan, son of Cairill, as we are told,
Was freed from sin by Jesus;
One hundred years complete he lived,
He lived in blooming manhood.

"2. Three hundred years in the shape of a wild ox
He lived on the open extensive plains;
Two hundred and five years he lived
In the shape of a wild boar.

---

[1] Diog Laert viii 12.

[2] De Bello Gallico, vi. 14. Compare Diodor. Sic v. 28.

"3. Three hundred years he was still in the flesh
In the shape of an old bird;
One hundred delightful years he lived
In the shape of a salmon in the flood.

"4. A fisherman caught him in his net,
He brought it to the king's palace;
When the bright salmon was there seen,
The queen immediately longed for it.

"5. It was forthwith dressed for her,
Which she alone ate entire;
The beauteous queen became pregnant,
The issue of which was Tuan."[1]

But the Book of Balimote is assigned by Irish scholars to the latter part of the 14th century;[2] and we may well be excused for a little scepticism as to the complete correctness of Cæsar's information respecting the Druids, when we find that it stands so altogether isolated, and that other details he gives about them are confessedly inaccurate.

---

[1] Tuan seems to have been a convert of Columkill (Columba), a sixth-century Irish saint —Celtic Scotland, a History of Ancient Albion, by William F Skene, 1880, Vol iii p 98

[2] My authority for this statement is a private letter from Professor Rhys, who refers to Eugene O Curry, Manners and Customs of the Ancient Irish, Vol. iii p. 60

Apart, however, from the Āryan races, the belief in the passage of the soul after death, not to another world only, but also into other human bodies in this world, is not uncommon, and has evidently had an independent origin in different times and countries. The various tribes of North-American Indians believed that the soul animating the body of an infant was the soul of some deceased person; enslaved negroes, according to Mr. Tylor, have been known to commit suicide, that they may revive in their native land; and the aborigines of Australia hold white men to be the manes or ghosts of their own dead. They are said to express this in the simple formula, "Black-fellow tumble down, "jump up White-fellow;" and a native hanged at Melbourne is represented to have given vent to the hopeful belief that he would "jump up White-fellow "and have lots of sixpences." I may add that the Jews, at different periods of their history, seem to have held a similar doctrine; for though I do not hold with those commentators who have discovered a reference to it in the New Testament, it is found distinctly in several parts of the Talmud.[1]

[1] John i. 21, ix. 2. Hershon's Talmudic Miscellany, pp 40, 57, 325—328, Goldstucker's Remains, &c, i 215. The alternative in John ix. 2, "Who did sin, this man or his parents, "that he should be born blind?" is one that would naturally occur to a Jew, who held, in the first place, that the "sins" of the parents

And souls are not supposed to come back only as men. Mr. Tylor shows how certain tribes in North and South America, and in various parts of Africa, "drawing no definite line of demarcation between the "souls of men and beasts, admit without difficulty the "transmission of human souls into the bodies of the "lower animals." We have seen above that similar ideas have been entertained, from time to time, by isolated thinkers in Egypt, Italy and Greece, and they may be found even in Christian countries. Origen, who was a Universal Restitutionist, speaks of a cognate theory; and in later times Descartes and Leibnitz and Lessing have leant in the same direction[1] And a learned author has drawn up a list of no less than 4977 books which treat, either in whole or in part, of the origin and destiny of the soul, and among these as many as 188 are on the Souls of Beasts.[2] Of these, I will only mention here two—quite lately published—a work by the well-known naturalist, the Rev. T. G.

---

were visited also upon the children, and, secondly, that sin was possible already in the womb, since the embryo, in its later stages, was possessed of consciousness See the speculations of the Rabbis referred to by Lightfoot in his comment on the verse The Augustinian theory of "peccatum originale" might equally give rise to such a question as the disciples are here represented to have put.

[1] See Appendix.

[2] Prof. Ezra Abbott's valuable Bibliography of the subject, annexed to William R Alger's Doctrine of a Future Life, New York, 1878

Wood, on Animals Here and Hereafter, and M. Louis Figuier's Le Lendemain de la Mort. Both of these teach the immortality of animals, and the French writer advocates a complete theory of transmigration.

---

Now we unfortunately have not, and can never hope to have, any information as to the ancient beliefs of the tribes who had entered India from the north-west before the Āryans, and whom the Āryans conquered and absorbed into their own community. Modern evidence of the beliefs now held among the hill tribes of India cannot be depended upon as affording any safe ground for conjecture in this respect; much less modern evidence as to the details of the Animism still current among their possibly distant relatives in other parts of the world, such as the Finns or Lapps. All that can be said is, that the Āryans did not bring a belief in transmigration of any kind with them into India. If, centuries before, they had ever entertained such ideas, which is wholly problematical, they had completely outgrown them. That they could have developed such ideas quite independently after their arrival in India, after the very different fancies recorded in the Vedas had become an accepted faith among them, is of course possible, but it is unlikely. No parallel instance could, at present at least, be adduced from religious history elsewhere; and had they done so, we should expect to find more distinct traces in the later pre-Buddhistic literature of the beginnings and gradual progress of the new theory. But the Brāhmanas still teach that the souls of men enter upon one new life—good or bad according to their conduct here—in the other worlds; and it is in rare passages of some of the earlier Upanishads that we first find the transmigration theory suddenly appearing in nearly perfect completeness [1]

Thus in the Chāndogya Upanishad, in a passage found also in the Brihad Āraṇyaka, we read: "Those "whose conduct has been good will quickly attain "some good birth, birth as a Brāhmana, or a Kshatriya, "or a Vaisya."[2]

And in the Kaushītaki Brāhmaṇa Upanishad: "All "who depart from this world go to the moon. In the "bright fortnight the moon is gladdened by their "spirits, but in the dark fortnight it sends them forth "into new births. Verily the moon is the door of "heaven. Him who rejects it, it sends on beyond; "but whoso rejects it not, him it rains down upon this "world. And here is he born either as a worm, or a "grasshopper, or a fish, or a bird, or a lion, or a boar,

[1] The theory occurs also in later Upanishads, such as the Garbha Up (Weber, Ind. Stud ii. pp 69, 70), but these are post-Buddhistic

[2] Chāndogya Upanishad, V 10 See Max Muller, Sacred Books of the East, Vol. i. p 84

"or a serpent, or a tiger, or a man, or some other "creature, according to his deeds and his knowledge."[1]

The belief in transmigration is here united with a notion that souls go first to the moon, a theory so curiously common that I have ventured to quote below some striking examples of it.[2] But we are concerned here only with the transmigration theory, and the passages now given show that that theory was already completely accepted in India at the time when these Upanishads were composed, which may be fixed approximately about 600 years before the Christian era. The absence of any trace of the theory before that time seems to me to point, as the most probable conclusion, to the hypothesis that the pre-Āryan occupants of the valley of the Ganges were believers in something of the kind, and that the Āryans first derived the principle of the idea from them; but not until long after the Āryans had entered India, and until the conquerors and the conquered had been fused together into one people.

---

At that time the schools of the philosophizing Brāhmans were already in full vigour; and though it is not easy to trace any modifications of the doctrine in pre-Buddhistic literature, it is quite possible that the idea

[1] Kaushītaki Brāhmana Upanishad, ed. Cowell, p. 146

[2] See Appendix.

as derived by the Āryans extended only to the return of men's souls to a new existence in the outward form of men, plants or animals; and that the Brāhmans themselves, or one or other of the heterodox teachers before Buddha, added the belief in the eternity of this transmigration, which has been so fundamental a part of the theory since the time of the rise of Buddhism. But Gotama himself may have added this part of the theory, for we have no clear evidence of it before he lived.

In this respect it would be well here to give some account of the general idea of transmigration as held in common throughout India by Hindūs after the fall of Buddhism. Parts of this belief may well be due to the influence of Buddhism, but it may also contain traces of ideas current when Buddhism arose, and of which we have no evidence from books known to be older than the time of Gotama. This general belief is, shortly stated, as follows

There is within the body of every man a soul, which, at the death of the body, flies away from it like a bird out of a cage, and enters upon a new life (at once, without going to the moon), either in one of the heavens, in one of the hells, or on this earth. The only exception is in the rare case of a man having in this life acquired a true knowledge of God. According to the pre-Buddhistic theory, the soul of such a man goes along the path of the gods to God, and being united with Him enters upon an immortal life in which his individuality is not extinguished. In the later theory, his soul is directly absorbed into the Great Soul, is lost in it, and has no longer any independent existence.

The souls of all other men enter, after the death of the body, upon a new existence in one or other of the many different modes of being. If in heaven or in hell, the soul itself becomes a god or a demon without entering a body; all superhuman beings, save the great gods, being looked upon as not eternal, but merely temporary creatures. If the soul returns to earth, it may, or may not, enter a new body; and this either of a human being, an animal, a plant, or even a material object. For all these are possessed of souls, and there is no essential difference between their souls and the souls of men—all being alike mere sparks of the Great Spirit, who is the only real existence.

The outward condition of the soul is, in each new birth, determined by its actions in a previous birth; but by each action in succession, and not by the balance struck after the evil has been reckoned off against the good. A good man who has once uttered a slander may spend a hundred thousand years as a god in consequence of his goodness, and, when the power of his good actions is exhausted, may be born as a dumb man on account of his transgression; and a robber, who has once done an act of mercy, may come to life in a king's body as the result of his virtue, and then suffer torments for ages in hell or as a ghost without a body, or be re-born many times as a slave or an outcast, in consequence of his evil life. The relation between the act and its fruit, between the *Karma* and its Vipāka, was practically looked upon as being so uncertain, undetermined and even arbitrary, that it is impossible to trace in ordinary cases any law or proportion between the cause and the effect. But the effect was considered to follow the cause inevitably and naturally, without the intervention of any deity to apportion the reward or punishment. And in special cases there was a vague feeling of a certain relation between the conduct and its result. Offences against the Brāhmans would unquestionably produce the most evil fruit with the greatest certainty and the greatest speed, and the performance of right sacrifices and liberality to the priests would in the shortest time bring about the happiest effect. All that was absolutely certain was that each act of the soul, good or bad, must work out its full effect to the sweet or bitter end.

There is no escape, according to this theory, from the result of any act; though it is only the consequences of its own acts that each soul has to endure. The force has been set in motion by itself, and can never stop; and its effect can never be foretold. If evil, it can never be modified or prevented, for it depends on a cause already completed, that is now for ever beyond the soul's control. There is even no continuing consciousness, no memory of the past that could guide the soul to any knowledge of its fate. The only advantage open to it is to add in this life to the sum of its good actions, that they may bear fruit with the rest. And even this can only happen in some future life under essentially the same conditions as the present one; subject, like the present one, to old age, decay and death; and affording opportunity, like the present one, for the commission of errors, ignorances or sins, which in their turn must inevitably produce their due effect of sickness, disability or woe. Thus is the soul tossed about from life to life, from billow to billow in the great ocean of transmigration. And there is no escape save for the very few who, during their birth as men, attain to a right knowledge of the Great Spirit; and thus enter into immortality, or, as the later philosophers taught, are absorbed into the Divine Essence.

---

As this theory is contradictory to ideas commonly held among us, it will be considered by many, without any further argument, to carry with it its own condemnation as a mere farrago of baseless fancies. The founder of Buddhism found something very like it an accepted belief, and he dealt with it as some Broadchurchmen deal with beliefs accepted now. He endeavoured to bring it into harmony with his new ideas by putting new meanings into the old phrases. And the extent of the modifications he introduced was determined by the method which he followed throughout the formulation of his whole system when he had to deal with the inherited beliefs. Like many earnest religious teachers of the present day, he did not leave them alone, and endeavour to arrive at truth by an examination of the evidence at his command, pausing humbly where incertitude began. But he rejected only those parts of his earliest creed which were clearly inconsistent with what he held to be true. In such cases, the ultimate beliefs accepted are not necessarily more true than those that are rejected; they are only less easily proved false.

Now the doctrine of a former existence, like the allied doctrine of a future life, cannot be disproved, for it deals with a sphere beyond the reach of human experience. And the doctrine that whatsoever a man reaps that he himself must also have sown, appealed as strongly to ethical natures as the very different, though allied, doctrine, that "whatsoever a man soweth that "shall he also reap," appeals to us now. These doctrines were retained by Gotama; and he also taught the eternal persistence in ordinary cases of the force of Karma. But he changed the whole aspect and practical effect of the doctrines he retained by disconnecting them from the soul-theory out of which they had grown and on which they had hitherto depended.

---

The various religious faiths professed in Europe are so inextricably interwoven with the belief in a soul, that it is very difficult in this respect rightly to appreciate the Buddhist point of view. We must never forget that the earliest Buddhism looks with a certain contempt and aversion on all these discussions about the future life. The Buddhist doctrine is: "Try to "get as near to wisdom and goodness as you can in "this life. Trouble not yourselves about the gods. "Disturb yourself not by curiosities or desires about "any future existence. Seek only after the fruit of "the noble path of self-culture and of self-control!"

Thus in the Sabbāsawa Sutta of the Majjhima Nikāya we read:

"It is by his consideration of those things which "ought not to be considered, and by his non-consider-"ation of those things which ought to be considered, "that wrong leanings of the mind, which had not "arisen before, arise within him; and wrong leanings "of the mind, which had arisen before, grow great!

"Unwisely doth he consider thus: 'Have I existed "'during the ages that are past, or have I not? What "'was I during the ages that are past? How was I "'during the ages that are past? Having been what, "'what did I become in the ages that are past? Shall "'I exist during the ages of the future, or shall I not? "'What shall I be during the ages of the future? "'How shall I be during the ages of the future? "'Having been what, what shall I become during the "'ages of the future?' Or he debates within himself "as to the present: 'Do I after all exist, or am I not? "'How am I? This is a being; whence now did it "'come, and whither will it go?'"

"In him thus unwisely considering, there springs "up one or other of the six absurd notions" [all of which are about the soul and are then set out]. "This, "brethren, is called the walking in delusion, the jungle, "the wilderness, the puppet-show, the writhing, the "fetter of delusion!" . . . .

"But the wise man, brethren, the disciple walking "in the noble path, who knows those who are walking "in the noble path, who comprehends, and is trained "according to the doctrine of the noble path . . . . "he understands both what things ought to be considered, and what things ought not to be considered. "And, thus understanding, the things that ought to "be considered, those he considers; and the things "that ought not to be considered, those he does not "consider."[1]

---

[1] Rh D Buddhist Suttas from the Pāli, pp 298—300

This sounds very much like the opinions we have lately become accustomed to hear labelled as Agnosticism. But any one who has read the Pāli Suttas will understand how Gotama would have rejected the epithet with an indignation none the less real for its mildness and benignity. His was essentially a positive, not a negative system. His objections to metaphysical discussions, or even musings, about the past or future conditions of the "soul," may be compared to the dislike of a practical politician, anxious to get on with arrears of work, to obstructive motions for the adjournment of the House. That those objections should be pitched upon as the characteristic mark of his opinions, as the appropriate ground for the name of his teaching, would have seemed to him ridiculous. Rightly or wrongly, he had an intense consciousness of insight; and so far from accepting the title of Agnostic, would have called himself, in the fullest possible sense, a Gnostic.

The unthinking multitude received, without a doubt, the soul-creed their fathers had held for hundreds, and probably for thousands, of years. The philosophers indulged in numberless speculations, which only agreed in regarding the subject as worth discussing. It is true he refused to follow their method, and refusal has a negative side. But in relation to them his position cannot rightly be called negative: it was the relation of the astronomer to the astrologer, of the chemist to the alchemist.

---

The parallelism of relation last referred to holds good also in other respects. History shows us that there was no sudden jump from folly to science, though the abandoning of vain hopes was a turning-point, a necessary step, in the progress of knowledge. Chemistry was the child of alchemy, and bore at first a strange likeness to its mother. So also Gotama, though he had reached the shore, stood where his feet were washed by the waves of the sea. That part of the then prevalent transmigration theory which could not be proved false seemed to meet a deeply-felt necessity, seemed to supply a moral cause which would explain the unequal distribution here of happiness or woe, so utterly inconsistent with the present characters of men. He still therefore talked of men's previous existence, but by no means in the way that he is generally represented to have done.

The transmigration of souls, very commonly supposed to be a fundamental part of Buddhism, has never been found mentioned at all, or even referred to, in the Pāli Piṭakas. I have no hesitation in maintaining, therefore, that Gotama did not teach the transmigration of souls. What he did teach would be better summarized, if we wish to retain the word transmigration, as the transmigration of character. But it would be more accurate to drop the word transmigration altogether when speaking of Buddhism, and to call its doctrine the doctrine of Karma. Gotama held that after the death of any being, whether human or not, there survived nothing at all but that being's "Karma," the result, that is, of its mental and bodily actions. Every individual, whether human or divine, was the last inheritor and the last result of the Karma of a long series of past individuals—a series so long that its beginning is beyond the reach of calculation, and its end will be coincident with the destruction of the world. From this it would follow that each generation was the exact, inevitable and natural result of the generation that had preceded it, that generation of the former one, and so on in succession during a practically endless past.

---

One of the latest speculations now being put forward among ourselves would seek to explain each man's character, and even his outward condition in life, by the character he inherited from his ancestors, a character gradually formed during a practically endless series of past existences, modified only by the conditions into which he was born, those very conditions being also in like manner the last result of a practically endless series of past causes. Gotama's speculation might be stated in the same words. But it attempted also to explain, in a way different from that which would be adopted by the exponents of the modern theory, that strange problem which it is also the motive of the wonderful drama of the Book of Job to explain—the fact that the actual distribution here of good fortune or misery is entirely independent of the moral qualities which men call good or bad. We cannot wonder that a teacher, whose whole system was so essentially an ethical reformation, should have felt it incumbent upon him to seek an explanation of this apparent injustice. And all the more so, since the belief he had inherited, the theory of the transmigration of souls, had provided a solution perfectly sufficient to any one who could accept that belief. In the older theory, it was the same soul that had done evil which suffered the penalty (or rather had to bear the inevitable consequence) of its wrongdoing; it was one and the same soul that did a good deed and that earned the reward (or rather that experienced the natural result of its goodness). In order to serve the moral cause, Gotama retained the idea of personal identity But he had discarded the theory of the presence, within each human body, of a soul which could have a separate and eternal existence[1] He therefore established a new identity between the

[1] See, on this point, below, Lecture VI

individuals in the chain of existence, which he, like his forerunners, acknowledged, by the new assertion that that which made two beings to be the same being was—not soul, but—Karma. He taught, as the modern speculation does, a real connection of cause and effect between persons in the present life and persons in a past life; but the connection was not a physical one between different individuals, it was a moral one between individuals who, according to the Buddhist belief, were the same.

The Christian would deny that the two persons are the same, for there is no continuing consciousness, no passage of a soul, or of an I in any sense, from the one to the other. The Evolutionist would say that the concentration in one new individual of the result of the Karma, the mental and bodily acts, of the one who has ceased to be, is no *vera causa*, but a pure hypothesis. But both will sympathize with the earnest seeking after a cause, and the overpowering sense of the necessity of justice, that gave rise to the formulation of the Buddhist belief. And the more thorough-going the Evolutionist, the more clear his vision of the long perspective of history, the greater will be his appreciation of the strangeness of the fact that a theory so far consistent with what he holds to be true should have been possible at all in so remote a past.

---

It is interesting to notice that the very point which is the weakness of the theory—the supposed concentration of the effect of the Karma in one new being—presented itself to the early Buddhists themselves as a difficulty. They avoided it partly by explaining that it was a particular thirst in the creature dying (a craving, Tanhā, which plays otherwise a great part in the Buddhist theory), which actually caused the birth of the new individual who was to inherit the Karma of the former one. But how this took place, how the craving desire produced this effect, was acknowledged to be a mystery patent only to a Buddha. I will not therefore dwell upon this further, except to point out the very curious coincidence that Plato, in adopting the Pythagorean transmigration into his system, added to it a very similar theory.

He makes Socrates say in the Phædo:[1]

"The truth rather is, that the soul which is pure at "departing and draws after her no bodily taint, having "never voluntarily had connection with the body, "which she is ever avoiding, herself gathered into "herself (for such abstraction has been the study of "her life: and what does this mean but that she has "been a true disciple of philosophy . . . .); that soul, "I say, herself invisible, departs to the invisible world,

---

[1] Phædo, 69 Jowett's Translation, i. 457, ed. 1875 For the context, see Appendix.

"to the divine and immortal and rational . . . . and is "released from the error and folly of men, their fears "and wild passions and all other human ills. . . . . But "the soul which has been polluted, and is impure at "the time of her departure, and is the companion and "servant of the body always, and is in love with and "fascinated by the body and by the desires and plea-"sures of the body, . . . . do you suppose that such a "soul will depart pure and unalloyed ?[1] . . . . She is "held fast by the corporeal, which the continual asso-"ciation and constant care of the body have wrought "into her nature, . . . . is depressed and dragged down "again into the visible world. These must be the "souls . . . . who are compelled . . . . to wander . . . . "in payment of the penalty of their former evil . . . . "until, through the craving after the corporeal "which never leaves them, they are imprisoned finally "in another body. And they may be supposed to find "their prisons in the same natures which they have had "in their former lives.[2] . . . . I mean to say that men "who have followed after gluttony, and wantonness, "and drunkenness, and have had no thought of avoid-"ing them, would pass into asses and animals of that "sort. . . . . And those who have chosen the portion of "injustice, and tyranny, and violence, will pass into "wolves, or into hawks and kites. . . . . And there is

---

[1] P 458. [2] P 459.

"no difficulty in assigning to all of them places accor-
"ding to their several natures and propensities. . . . .
"Even among them, some are happier than others;
"and the happiest, both in themselves and their place
"of abode, are those who have practised the civil and
"social virtues which are called temperance and justice,
"and are acquired by habit and attention, without
"philosophy and mind. . . . . Because they may be
"expected to pass into some gentle social nature which
"is like their own, such as that of bees or wasps or ants,
"or even back again into the form of man, and just and
"moderate men to spring from them. . . . . But he who
"is a philosopher or lover of learning, and is entirely
"pure at departing, is alone permitted to attain to the
"divine nature."

Plato, it is true, lays down in this passage a theory which, in a very fundamental part of it, the assertion of the existence of souls within men's bodies, is diametrically opposed to the Buddhist theory; and even with regard to the action of desire, he does not go as far as the great Indian teacher. Gotama held that it was equally desire which brought about, not only a new existence as an animal, but also as a man or a god. But when we find that the two greatest ethical thinkers of antiquity have independently arrived at conclusions so very similar, have agreed in ascribing to desires entertained in this life so great, and to us so inconceivable, a power over the future life, we may well hesitate before we condemn the idea as intrinsically absurd. I would submit that we must go further, and acknowledge in this curious coincidence another very striking instance of the most important fact which the comparative study of Buddhism has to show,—I mean the fact, that, given similar conditions, similar stages in the course of religious inquiry, men's thoughts, even in spite of the most unquestioned individual originality, and though they have never produced quite the same results, have constantly tended in similar directions.

---

This curious parallel—which, whatever the conclusion to be drawn from it, will, I trust, be thought worthy to have been pointed out—may throw some light upon the Buddhist theory. Life, according to that theory, is a chain of existences, never ending, and the sequences of which can never be foretold. It follows, firstly, that it will be good to escape from the chain, to attain to a condition that will be outside of the circle of change, outside the reach of the causes of change, and that will contain within itself the element of finality.

The only such condition is, according to Buddhism, that state of mind, to be reached in this life, in which the craving desire just spoken of shall have ceased. No new link will then be formed in the chain of existence; the Karma of that particular chain of lives will cease to influence any longer any distinct individual; and there will be no more birth; for birth, decay and death, grief, lamentation and despair, will have come, so far as regards that chain of lives, for ever to an end.

Now that state of mind is nothing else than Arahatship. So that our discussion, as every right discussion of any part of Buddhism ought to do, has brought us to that central point of the Buddha's teaching, the goal, the hope, the aim of every good and enlightened Buddhist, the "Excellent Way" of self-culture and of self-control.

As is said in the account of the closing days of Gotama's life, "the Blessed One addressed the disciples of Bhandagāma, and said,[1]

"It is through not understanding and grasping four "conditions (four things), O Brethren, that we have "had to run so long, to wander so long, in this weary "path of individuality, both you and I.

"And what are these four?

"The noble conduct of life, the noble earnestness in "meditation, the noble kind of wisdom, and the noble "salvation of freedom. But when the noble kind of "conduct of life, of earnestness in meditation, of wisdom, "and of salvation by freedom, are seen face to face, "and are comprehended, then is the craving for exist-

[1] Book of the Great Decease (iv 2, 3) Rh D, Buddhist Suttas from the Pāli, pp 64, 65

"ence rooted out, that which leads to renewed exist-
"ence is destroyed, and there is no more birth.

"Righteousness, earnest thought, wisdom and freedom sublime,
"These are the truths realized by Gotama far renowned.
"Knowing them, he, the Knower, proclaimed the truth to the brethren.
"The Master, with eye divine, the Quencher of griefs, is free!"

The four Dhammas or conditions called in this passage noble, are only one of many descriptions of what constitutes Arahatship, the end of the so-called Noble Path. But we cannot enlarge here upon Arahatship, or the Noble Path. I can only say now that it has many sides and many names, and that it is in reference to this extinction of that foolish and ignorant three-fold craving—the lust of the flesh, the lust of life, and the pride of life—and of the three most immediate results of that craving—viz. the inward fires of lust, hatred and delusion—that Arahatship is called Nibbāna or Nirvaṇa, a word which means "the going out, the becoming extinct," and has often, therefore, by writers ignorant of the first principles of Buddhism, been supposed to mean the extinction of the soul! It is the "going out" of craving (Tanhā) and of the three fires just referred to.

It follows that a good Buddhist must love righteousness for its own sake, and not for any supposed benefit that will accrue to him himself in a future life on account of his righteousness. For Buddhism does not teach any conscious identity between any two links in the chain of life, and it holds that the perfection of goodness and wisdom will actually put an end at once and irrevocably to any continuation at all of the good man's life in any sense.

As the Buddhist writers are fond of saying, the relation of the one life to the next is merely like that borne by the flame of a lamp to the flame of another lamp lighted by it. When the Arahat, the man made perfect according to the Buddhist faith, ceases to live, no new lamp, no new sentient being, will be lighted by the flame of any weak or ignorant longing entertained by him. Alice in Wonderland puts the point exactly when she asks the question, full of the delicious naiveté and confusion of a child's metaphysic, "I wonder—what the flame of a candle looks like after the candle's gone out?" It looks, according to early Buddhism, exactly like what little Alice and you and I will look like when our heart has ceased to beat, when the temporary collocation and combination of those Saŋkhāras, those Confections, whose union makes our temporary individuality, shall have been dissolved; when our life has closed for ever, and our opportunities of personal culture and happiness, our opportunities of kindness and of love, our opportunities of public service, our opportunities of service to the generations yet unborn, shall have passed away, never to revive in any different world!

This is in instructive contrast to the teachings of the theologies which hold out the hope, or state as a matter of fact, that a life of goodness or of right faith here on earth will render possible the inheritance of an immortality of heavenly bliss; and which then, logically enough, insist, in the way of consolation and support, upon the utter shortness of the struggle as compared with the unspeakable infinity of the bliss beyond. In Buddhism, however exalted the virtue, however clear the insight, however humble the faith, there is no Arahatship if the mind be still darkened by any hankering after any kind of future life.

---

This is clear from the passage just read from the Book of the Great Decease, and also from the description, quoted above in the first Lecture, of the virtue of the Arahat as Aparamaṭṭho, "untarnished;" that is, untarnished by faith in the efficacy of ritual or by desire for future life.[1] We cannot be surprised to find,

[1] Book of the Great Decease, i 11, ii 9, and frequently elsewhere. See above, p. 29, where the context is quoted.

therefore, that this desire for a future life constitutes, two, out of a total of ten, Saŋyojanas, or "fetters," of the mind, to have broken loose from which constitutes the "noble salvation of freedom" reached, in this life, in Arahatship. So the Cetokhila Sutta calls the entertainment of this desire after future life "spiritual "bondage," and adds,

"Whatsoever brother, O Bhikkhus, may have left "the world to enter the Order in the aspiration of be-"longing to some one or other of the angel hosts, think-"ing to himself, 'By this morality, by this observance, "'by this austerity, or by this earnestness of life, "'may I become an angel, or one of the angels!' his "mind inclineth not to zeal, exertion, perseverance and "struggle. But whosever mind inclineth not to zeal, "exertion, perseverance and struggle, he has not broken "through this Fifth Spiritual Bondage. . . . . And "whatsoever brother, O Bhikkhus, has not become "quite free from the five kinds of spiritual barrenness, "has not altogether broken through the five kinds of "mental bondage—that such an one should reach up "to the full advantage of, should attain to full growth "in this doctrine and discipline—that can in no wise "be!"[1]

So that not only is the Arahat to look for no reward, no happiness, which he himself is to be conscious of

[1] Rh. D, Buddhist Suttas from the Pāli, pp 227, 228, where the context may be seen

hereafter, but the nourishing of any hope of a future life is really even worse than unfounded; it is declared to be an actual impediment in the way of the only object that we ought to seek after, viz. the attainment in this world of the state of mental and ethical culture summed up in the word Arahatship.

---

It is easy to understand that this adaptation and modification of the previously existing doctrine of the transmigration of souls had little chance of being received with enthusiasm, or even approval, among a populace accustomed to Animistic ideas much more congenial to the natural man. They preferred to look for a better world beyond, which the ritualisms would ensure to them, and to which the theologies could guide them. Now early Buddhism had its answer also to them, and it was this: Very good; you want to go to heaven. It is really a mistake. Arahatship is better than heaven, and the Arahats are above all gods. But still, if you cannot comprehend that, then at least understand that the only way to heaven is—not ritual, but—righteousness.

There is very clear distinction drawn by some Christian teachers between the goodness of a converted Christian and the mere natural goodness of a moral man. A similar distinction runs all through the early

Buddhist teachings between the intelligent goodness of those who have entered the Excellent Way, and the lower kind of goodness attainable by ordinary men. It is this lower kind of goodness which leads to re-birth in blissful states. And though the new being, according to the doctrine of the creative force of Craving Desire and of the transfer of Karma, will not be consciously the same as the man who dies, it will be, according to Buddhism, really the same, for it will inherit the same Karma.

To the unconverted good man, then, the hope of a temporary life in heaven is as really held out in Buddhism as the hope of an eternal life in heaven is held out to the converted good man in Christianity. And in the same way the fear of purgatory, of a temporary fall into hell, is used as an argument in Buddhism to deter ordinary men from evil, just as the fear of purgatory is made use of among the Catholics, and the fear of hell among both Catholics and evangelical Protestants.

---

It is very curious to notice that re-birth as an animal, which is of course possible according to the Buddhist theory, is scarcely ever referred to in this connection. We constantly find re-birth in general referred to as an evil, heaven and purgatory spoken of as the places to which the good and the evil respectively go, or life in the next world, the other world, represented as following, for all persons not Arahats, after life in this.

So in the Book of the Great Decease, Gotama is represented, when giving milk to babes, to have said that "the wrong-doer . . . . on the dissolution of the "body, after death, is re-born into some unhappy state "of suffering and woe." While "the well-doer, on "the dissolution of the body, after death, is re-born "into some happy state in heaven."[1] Other similar passages are as follows:

"There also do his good works receive him who has "done good, and has gone from this world to the "other—as kinsmen receive a favourite on his return.[2]

"When a man becomes fat and a great eater, a "sluggard, rolling this way and that as he lies, like a "great hog fed on offerings to the gods—again and "again does that fool enter the womb."[3]

"Him indeed I call a Brāhmaṇa who knows his "former abodes, who sees through heaven and hell, "who has reached the end of births."[4]

"He having mounted the Devayāna (the vehicle of "the gods, exactly as in the Upanishads) and entered

---

[1] Rh. D., Buddhist Suttas, &c, pp 16, 17.

[2] Dhammapadaŋ, verse 220.

[3] Ibid. verse 325.

[4] Sutta Nipāta, verse 647, repeated in Dhammapadaŋ, verse 423.

"the high road that is free from dust, having aban-
"doned sensual desires, went to the Brahma world."[1]

"Those beings who are possessed of form, and those "who dwell in the formless worlds (that is, the highest "heavens), have to go to re-birth, for they know not "Arahatship.

"But those who, having seen through all forms, who "are made free in Arahatship, such beings leave death "behind."[2]

The one connection in which re-birth as an animal is incidentally referred to, is when speaking of a Sotāpanno, an Ariya-sāvako, who has entered the Noble Path, but has stopped short in his journey along it. He is represented to be "free from re-birth" in five kinds of various unhappy states (the pañca-gatiyo), of which that of being an animal is mentioned as one.[3]

I trust I shall not be misunderstood. It is a question of degree. Re-birth as an animal, that is to say, the transfer of a man's Karma to an animal, either immediately or after some intervening stage, is clearly part of the oldest Buddhist belief. And the authors of later works rightly take it for granted. In the Cariyā Piṭaka, which is even included in the supplementary part of the Pāli Piṭakas, the Karma of the

---

[1] Sutta Nipāta, verse 138.

[2] Ibid 754, 755

[3] See Appendix for the authorities for this statement.

future Buddha is represented to have belonged, and apparently in succession, both to men and to animals. And certainly the Jātaka stories, though only in one or two isolated instances, speak of the Karma of a human being being immediately transferred to an animal.[1] But not a single instance has been found in the older parts of the Pāli Piṭakas of a man being re-born as an animal, and, with the single exception just referred to, the doctrine is not even alluded to.

It is strange that this has never been yet pointed out, for it seems to me to be of considerable importance for a right understanding of the early Buddhist belief. It has been so commonly supposed that the transmigration of the souls of men into animals was one of the principal, perhaps the most distinguishing characteristic of Buddhism, that I am afraid I must seem somewhat of an iconoclast in maintaining, not merely that there is no transmigration of souls in Gotama's teaching, that his real theory is a transfer of Karma, but even that comparatively little stress was originally laid upon the possibility of this transfer of Karma taking place immediately from a man to an animal.

Yet you will recollect that the Upanishads say the souls of all dead men go to the moon, and thence only descend on to earth or into animals. In harmony with

---

[1] See, for instance, Rh. D., Buddhist Birth Stories, Vol. i. p. 258.

this, the earliest Buddhist doctrine may very well have been that the Karma of unconverted men would ordinarily be carried on by new beings in one of the various heavens or purgatories, and that only after this intermediate state of existence had come to an end would their Karma be again carried on by other beings, including animals. It is at all events certain that any such birth in purgatory, or as an animal, was rendered impossible by the very entrance upon the Path, by the getting rid of the "fetter" of the delusions regarding the persistence of individuality; while the attainment of Arahatship in this life at once prevented the Karma from being carried on by any individual of any kind whatever.

---

In no case is there, therefore, any future life in the Christian sense. At a man's death, nothing survives but the effect of his actions; and the good that he has done, though it lives after him, will redound, not to his own benefit, as we should call it, but to the benefit of generations yet unborn, between himself and whom there will be no consciousness of identity in any shape or way.

As has been well pointed out by the Rev. Dr. Dods in his interesting work entitled, Mohammed, Buddha and Christ, "This is the Buddhist analogue to the

"Positivist offset to personal annihilation so winningly "presented by George Eliot:

"'O may I join the choir invisible
Of those immortal dead who live again
In minds made better by their presence: live
In pulses stirred to generosity,
In deeds of daring rectitude, in scorn
For miserable aims that end with self,
In thoughts sublime that pierce the night like stars,
And with their mild persistence urge men's search
To vaster issues . . . .
. . . . . This is life to come!'"

There is doubtless some analogy between this beautiful sentiment and the Buddhist doctrine. But the modern poet has her mind directed upon the future, and the ancient prophet is thinking more especially of the past. Early Buddhism had no idea, just as early Christianity had not, of the principle underlying the foundation of the higher morality of the future, the duty which we owe, not only to our fellow-men of to-day, but also to those of the morrow—to the race as a whole, but in the future even more than now. Buddhists and Christians may both maintain, and rightly maintain, that the duty of universal love laid down in their Scriptures can be held to involve and include this modern conception; but neither the early Buddhists nor the early Christians looked at the matter quite in this way. The sense of duty to the race has sprung out of a fact, only lately become a generally received conception—I mean the progressive continuity of human progress. And the corresponding doctrine of Buddhism is not that "the thoughts of men are "widened with the process of the suns," but that there are recurring cycles of improvement and decay.

It is true that the Buddhist duty of universal love is much more far-reaching as regards the present than the corresponding duty as commonly received in any other religion. It enfolds in its ample embrace not only the brethren and sisters of the new faith, not only our neighbours, but every being that has life. "As a mother, even at the risk of her own life, "protects her son, her only son, so let a man cultivate "goodwill without measure toward all beings. "Let him cultivate goodwill without measure—unhin-"dered love and friendliness—toward the whole world, "above, below, around. Standing, walking, sitting or "lying, let him be firm in this mind so long as he is "awake: this state of heart, they say, is the best in "the world!"[1]

But, so far as I know, it never occurred to the Bud-

[1] Brahmaŋ vihāraŋ idha, literally "the highest condition" It is more fully described in the passage quoted at the close of the last Lecture from the Tevijja Sutta. The verses here quoted are from the Metta Sutta, which forms part both of the Khuddaka Pātha, and of the Sutta Nipāta.

dhist teachers to inculcate a duty towards the beings that will exist in the ages yet to come. Even such passages as that from the Sūtra of the Forty-two Sections, "To give food to such by the thousand myriad is "not like giving food to one Buddha, and learning to "pray to him from a desire to save all living creatures," have not been found as yet in the older books. The expression "pray to him" is certainly impossible Buddhism even at the date of the Sūtra of the Forty-two Articles, and evidently rests on a mistranslation.[1]

It is interesting to notice, however, how the glamour of the old Animism still survives both in the Buddhist doctrine and in George Eliot's poetry. Both hold that there is not really any "life to come" at all, in the ordinary Animistic sense; that all that survives is Karma. But both put the new wine into the old bottles. Both wrap up the bitter pill of absolute personal dissolution in the sweetmeat of the old familiar phrases, for the better presentation of their new truth to egoistic minds, still hampered by what Gotama's disciples called the Sakkāya-diṭṭhi, Bhavāsavā, the taint, the delusion, of the hankering after a continuing individuality.

[1] It occurs in Mr Beal's "Catena of Buddhist Scriptures from the Chinese" M. Foucaux, in his "Sutra en 42 Articles" (Paris, 1878, p 15), gives an entirely different, and no doubt more accurate version, direct from the original Sanskrit He translates the last clause, "Cela est ainsi à cause du desir de rechercher, d'apprendre "à fond la voie du Bouddha, et de procurer le bien de tous les êtres"

And both, I think, were a little, just a little, caught in their own net. Did not the gifted poet see a something more than poetic play of words in her "life to "come"? And certainly, however often "the Master "with eye divine" reiterated, when speaking of the Arahat, the praises of individual cessation, both he and Plato attached to desire, as a real and sober fact, an influence and a power which has no actual existence.

---

There is one other comparison which will help us to understand, not only the Buddhist theory of pre-existence, but beliefs more familiar to us which have played a very great part in human affairs I mean, firstly, that sense of an overruling and arbitrary Fate so powerfully represented in the Greek tragedies, and still so powerful among many peoples (more especially among Muhammadans); and secondly, that doctrine of predestination, of the foreknowledge of God, which has occupied so large a space in the thoughts of many Christian men. Each of these theories endeavours to give a philosophical explanation of an undeniable fact, the presence within us and about us of an irresistible power, which cannot be traced, and from which there is no escape.

The Muhammadan doctrine of fate is not mere confession of ignorance, mere giving up in despair. It includes a humble submission, a patient resignation, which is often the best medicine for the supposed malady. Predestination is the logical expression, from the Monotheistic point of view, of the weight of the universe arrayed against the individual. Pre-existence, that part of the transmigration of Karma which is predominantly insisted upon in early Buddhism, is an ethical meeting of the same difficulty.

The fact underlying all these theories is acknowledged to be a very real one. The history of the individual does not begin with his birth. He has been endless generations in the making. And he cannot sever himself from his surroundings; no, not for an hour. The tiny snowdrop droops its fairy head just so much, and no more, because it is balanced by the universe. It is a snowdrop, not an oak, and just that kind of snowdrop, because it is the outcome of the Karma of an endless series of past existences; and because it did not begin to be when the flower opened, or when the mother-plant first peeped above the ground, or first met the embraces of the sun, or when the bulb began to shoot beneath the soil, or at any time which you or I can fix. A great American writer says: "It "was a poetic attempt to lift this mountain of Fate, to "reconcile this despotism of race with liberty, when "the Hindoos said, 'Fate is nothing but the deeds "'committed in a prior state of existence.' I find the "coincidence of Eastern and Western speculation in "the daring statement of the German philosopher "Schelling, 'There is in every man a certain feeling "'that he has been what he is from all eternity.'" We may put a new and deeper meaning into the words of the poet:

.... "Our deeds follow us from afar,
And what we have been makes us what we are."

---

As in the older teaching, so in modern Buddhism, it is this pre-existence aspect of the theory which plays the greatest part and has the greatest vitality. The modern Buddhist rarely imagines, or is afraid, that there is any chance of his being re-born as an animal. He may think of such an event with regard to his neighbour, or as a joke, but not in a serious, religious mood as a possible occurrence to himself. The doctrine of Karma was never intended to be so much an explanation of what would happen to men after death, as an explanation, drawn from the past, of what was now happening to him during life. And so also the belief in previous existence still presents itself to the Buddhist as a theory which accounts for the present by the past, and as the foundation of the humorous ethics, the sly fun, of the Buddhist Birth Stories.

These are still and always have been a very present reality, a great power, to the vast numbers of the

Buddhists in every land. I recollect, some years ago, when I was in Ceylon, riding one night along the beautiful road from Galle to Colombo, one of the most lovely roads in the world, shaded throughout with the exquisite roof of the palm-leaves, and bordered on one side with long stretches of green sward clearly visible between the branchless stems of the trees, while on the other side the blue sea beats upon the shore, and bears with it a fresh and strengthening breeze. The moon was bright—more full than usual, I suppose, with the radiance of the departed souls of the good;—and at a turn of the road I came suddenly in view of an open space, visible through the trees on my left, where hundreds of people, dressed in their best and brightest, were seated on the ground, listening to what appeared to be a sermon. I rode up, and was surprised to find them talking and smiling pleasantly to one another. Tired with my journey, I stopped and listened. What they were drinking in with such evident delight were Jātaka tales, the Buddhist Birth Stories. This day, too, we have had a long journey, and we are perhaps somewhat like Milton's angels who

> "reasoned high
> Of providence, foreknowledge, will and fate,
> Fixed fate, free will, foreknowledge absolute,
> And found no end in wandering mazes lost."

Will you let us rest ourselves for awhile, while you

listen to a Jātaka story which is very much to the point?

"Long ago the Bodisat was born to a forest life as "Genius of a tree standing near a certain lotus pond.

"Now at that time the water used to run short at "the dry season in a certain pond, not over large, in "which there were a good many fish. And a crane "thought, on seeing the fish—

"'I must outwit these fish somehow or other and "'make a prey of them.'

"And he went and sat down at the edge of the "water, thinking how he should do it.

"When the fish saw him, they asked him, 'What "'are you sitting there for, lost in thought?'

"'I am sitting thinking about you,' said he.

"'Oh, sir! what are you thinking about us?' said "they.

"'Why,' he replied, 'there is very little water in "'this pond, and but little for you to eat; and the "'heat is so great! So I was thinking, What in the "'world will these fish do now?'

"'Yes, indeed, sir! what *are* we to do?' said they.

"'If you will only do as I bid you, I will take you "'in my beak to a fine large pond, covered with all "'the kinds of lotuses, and put you into it,' answered "the crane

"'That a crane should take thought for the fishes

" 'is a thing unheard of, sir, since the world began. " 'It's eating us, one after the other, that you're aiming " 'at!'

" 'Not I! So long as you trust me, I won't eat " 'you. But if you don't believe me that there is such " 'a pond, send one of you with me to go and see it.'

"Then they trusted him, and handed over to him "one of their number—a big fellow, blind of one eye, "whom they thought sharp enough in any emergency, "afloat or ashore.

"Him the crane took with him, let him go in the "pond, showed him the whole of it, brought him back, "and let him go again close to the other fish. And "he told them all the glories of the pond.

"And when they heard what he said, they ex-"claimed, 'All right, sir! You may take us with " 'you.'

"Then the crane took the old purblind fish first to "the bank of the other pond, and alighted in a Varaṇa-"tree growing on the bank there. But he threw it "into a fork of the tree, struck it with his beak and "killed it, and then ate its flesh, and threw its bones "away at the foot of the tree. Then he went back "and called out—

" 'I've thrown that fish in; let another come!'

"And in that manner he took all the fish, one by "one, and ate them, till he came back and found no "more!

"But there was still a crab left behind there; and "the crane thought he would eat him too, and called "out—

"'I say, good crab, I've taken all the fish away, and "'put them into a fine large pond. Come along; I'll "'take you too!'

"'But how will you take hold of me to carry me "'along?'

"'I'll bite hold of you with my beak.'

"'You'll let me fall if you carry me like that. I "'won't go with you.'

"'Don't be afraid! I'll hold you quite tight all "'the way.'

"Then said the crab to himself, 'If this fellow once "'got hold of fish, he would never let them go in a "'pond! Now if he should really put me into the "'pond, it would be capital; but if he doesn't—then "'I'll cut his throat and kill him!' So he said to "him—

"'Look here, friend; you won't be able to hold me "'tight enough; but we crabs have a famous grip. "'If you let me catch hold of you round the neck with "'my claws, I shall be glad to go with you.'

"And the other did not see that he was trying to "outwit him, and agreed. So the crab caught hold "of his neck with his claws as securely as with a pair "of blacksmith's pincers, and called out, 'Off with '"you, now!'

"And the crane took him and showed him the pond, "and then turned off towards the Varaṇa-tree.

"'Uncle!' cried the crab, 'the pond lies that way, "'but you are taking me this way!'

"'Oh, that's it, is it!' answered the crane. 'Your "'dear little uncle, your very sweet nephew, you call "'me! You mean me to understand, I suppose, that "'I am your slave, who has to lift you up and carry "'you about with him! Now cast your eye upon "'the heap of fish-bones lying at the root of yonder "Varaṇa-tree! Just as I have eaten those fish, every "'one of them, just so I will devour you as well!'

"'Ah! those fishes got eaten through their own "'stupidity,' answered the crab; 'but I'm not going "'to let you eat *me*. On the contrary, it is *you* that "'I am going to destroy. For you in your folly have "'not seen that I was outwitting you. If we die, we "'die both together; for I will cut off this head of "'yours and cast it to the ground!' And so saying, "he gave the crane's neck a grip with his claws, as "with a vice.

"Then, gasping, and with tears trickling from his "eyes, and trembling with the fear of death, the crane "beseeched him, saying, 'O, my Lord! Indeed I did "'not intend to eat you! Grant me my life!'

"'Well, well! step down into the pond, and put "'me in there.'

"And he turned round and stepped down into the

"pond, and placed the crab on the mud at its edge. "But the crab cut through its neck as clean as one "would cut a lotus-stalk with a hunting-knife, and "then only entered the water!

"When the Genius who lived in the Varana-tree saw "this strange affair, he made the wood resound with "his plaudits, uttering in a pleasant voice the verse—

"The villain, though exceeding clever,
Shall prosper not by his villany.
He may win indeed, sharp-witted in deceit,
But only as the Crane here from the Crab!"

These things are an allegory. De te fabula, lector carissime, narratur. The shallow pond is the world; the fishes are mankind; the fine large pond is security, salvation; the crane, who has grown up with the fishes and is nourished by them, is the prevalent superstition, the inherited belief; the old purblind fish—he is quite well-meaning and honest—is the priest; and the crab, with the tight grasp of truth, is as the Arahat, the man made free by insight, who cuts off the head of delusion "as clean as one would cut a lotus-stalk with a hunting-knife," and then only enters into the calm waters of security.[1]

---

[1] On this interpretation of the fable, compare Sutta Nipāta, verses 777, 936

## LECTURE IV.

# BUDDHIST LIVES OF THE BUDDHA.

---

One of the most valuable results to be gleaned from a study of Buddhism is a knowledge of the methods by which the early Buddhists attempted to give expression to the deep impression of a force of character, and of a wisdom beyond their ken, produced in their minds by the striking personality of Gotama.

To understand those methods, and to appreciate the lessons they convey, we must transport ourselves in imagination to the fifth century before the birth of Christ, and keep constantly before our minds the intellectual conditions among which the early Buddhists moved. Thus only shall we be able to follow the perfectly natural course of the growth of ideas concerning a perfectly natural man, whom the orthodox Buddhists came eventually to regard as a being quite different from ordinary men, and endowed with powers quite different from theirs.

An attempt has often been made to draw a curious

conclusion from the supposed fact that the date at which the Buddha flourished coincides pretty nearly with that of Pythagoras, Confucius and Zoroaster. The conclusion is, that the rise at the same time, quite independently, and in such distant lands, of four great religious thinkers and reformers, can only have been due to a certain wave of spiritual feeling then passing over the world. If this is a mere figure of speech, it is not very happily chosen, for it is both self-contradictory and misleading. It suggests an occult influence making itself felt across the earth, and contradicts the very hypothesis on which it rests, that the movements were independent; and it hides from view the probable explanation of so much of truth as lies behind the loose statement that these teachers were contemporaneous. A more accurate chronology, even when stated in round numbers, would show that Pythagoras was a century before Confucius, Confucius a century before Gotama, and Zoroaster of a date quite uncertain, but probably older than any of the three. The kind of electric thrill which our figure supposes must have been of a peculiarly wayward kind. Starting from Persia, it travels slowly to Greece, rests there for a time, returns across Persia and Mongolia (leaving them uninfluenced by its path) till it comes to China, and then returns, after a lapse of time which gives but small proof of vitality, to India. But the figure gives expression, however unsuccessfully, to a real connection which is no figure of speech,—a connection, not of actual contact by spiritual thrill or otherwise, but of similarity in origin. The religious movements, emphasized in these different countries by the careers of these four reformers, came after, and in consequence of, a long series of previous movements. And these previous movements were in fact so similar that they ran along nearly parallel lines resting on the common basis of Animistic conceptions. And similar causes acting in these parallel lines took about, though by no means exactly, the same time to produce corresponding results.

What that line of developement had been in India, we have endeavoured in previous Lectures to show. The rough science and childish philosophy of Animism had been moulded, in much the same way as it had been elsewhere, and notably in Greece, into that strange Pantheism of the Upanishads which, though we may not agree with it, we must acknowledge to be one of the most interesting records of honest and fearless inquiry handed down to us from ancient times. There were different schools of thought among these Pantheistic philosophers, but the various schools were all paths to the same city. But it seems as if, in proportion as the philosophers became more thorough-going in their new conceptions, the theologians and the people became more superstitious. For the Brāhman philosophers, like the French abbés of the last century, had not the honesty and the boldness to secede openly from the accepted belief; and ethics were as yet quite distinct from religion, which was chiefly concerned with forms of ritual[1] Outside ritual and philosophy, the dwellers in the valley of the Ganges had little mental food. The poetical side of the hymns of the Vedas had become obscured, the epics and the drama of later times were as yet unborn, and the charms of scientific or historical inquiry were quite unknown.

---

There then appeared the teacher of a new religion, pre-eminently ethical, anti-ritualistic, and even anti-philosophical. For though Gotama was highly trained in the current systems of philosophy, he studied them only, like Hume, to show their unreliability. And he taught that dabbling in metaphysics and speculation was a hindrance, not a help, to that inward growth which was the only thing he held to be worth striving for.

The little that can be ascertained of his real life will be known to any of those present who may have read my manual of "Buddhism." Will they excuse me if I recapitulate in a few sentences, for those who have not, the principal facts.

---

[1] Compare what has been well said by Mr Cust, Linguistic and Oriental Essays, p 113

Gotama was the son of a rāja, a kind of petty chieftain of the Sākya clan, who were settled some hundred miles north of the Ganges, on the spurs at the foot of the Himālaya range. The date of his birth is not quite certain, as the oldest authority on the point, the Dīpavaŋsa, gives two inconsistent accounts of the period that elapsed between his time and that of Asoka. But it can be fixed with sufficient accuracy at between the middle and the end of the sixth century B.C., a period during which the conditions of the valley of the Ganges underwent no material change. He was married in early youth to his first cousin, the daughter of the rāja over the neighbouring clan of the Koliyans, whose principal village was only a few miles from the village of Kapila-vatthu, in which he was born. We hear nothing more till his twenty-ninth year, when, after a long spiritual struggle, the causes and the nature of which we may guess at, but shall never exactly know, he finally abandoned his home. After first studying under teachers of repute, from whom he derived no satisfactory solution of the problems of life, he devoted himself for six years to the strictest penance, by which men then thought that they could obtain the mastery over the gods. Though his efforts in this direction were such, that we are told of his fame having spread abroad like the sound of a great bell hung in the skies, this also led to no lasting peace. And in his thirty-fifth year he passed through a second great mental crisis, the details of which, as described in Buddhist books with all the poetry the Indian mind was at that time master of, are curiously similar to those of the temptation in the wilderness. The end of this struggle was reached when, under the famous Bo-tree at Buddha Gayā, he attained to that state of mind which was afterwards called Buddhahood, and found at last a final solution of all his doubts and all his difficulties in the power over the human heart of inward self-culture and of love to all other beings.

After a struggle with the not unnatural hesitation whether it would be of any use to make these views known to others, he decided to proclaim publicly the truth he thought he had discovered; and for forty-five years he walked from place to place in the valley of the Ganges publishing the good news, and gathering round him a small band of earnest and faithful followers, the earliest members of his afterwards famous Order. At last, having gained a considerable measure of success, he died peacefully, in the midst of his disciples, in his eightieth year, at Kusi-nagara in Vesāli, not very far beyond the Ganges from the scene of his early studies.

Such are the simple facts of the career of the man whose life has been more momentous in its influence upon a large proportion of the human race than that of any other man who has ever lived. But is this the view of Gotama's life which has been recorded by his disciples in the Buddhist books themselves?

The analogy of similar records in the case of other religious founders, would lead us to expect that the followers of the great Indian teacher would not be satisfied by looking upon their master as a mere ordinary man; and this expectation is abundantly fulfilled. They endeavoured to give expression to their deep feelings of homage and of hero-worship, to their deep sense of inferiority, to the deep impression made upon them by the personal power of a character quite unequalled among all the men they knew or heard of, by describing the glory and the grandeur of their Buddha in poetical and figurative language always liable to be misunderstood, and hardening too soon into erroneous beliefs.

When we call to mind how great was the similarity of the outward conditions under which Christianity and Buddhism arose, how strikingly analogous in many respects were the mental qualities of the early Christians to those of the early Buddhists, how closely the personal feelings of the first Christian disciples to the Christ resembled those of the first Buddhist disciples to the Buddha, we are naturally very strongly interested to learn what was the effect in the case of early Buddhism of causes which must also have operated in the history of early Christianity. But the value of the comparison will be lost unless we bear also in mind the many differences in the two cases, as well as their resemblances. We must no more expect to find that the histories of early Buddhist and early Christian beliefs as to the person of their respective teachers will be, even in the smallest statement, exactly the same, than we expect to find that the growth of Pantheism out of Polytheism, in the valley of the Ganges and on the shores of the Mediterranean, was in all respects identical. We have to deal merely with similarities, not with identities.

---

The early Buddhist ideas of the Buddha were chiefly modified by two ideals dominating the minds of men in those days, neither of which had any necessary connection with the particular individual whom we know by the name of Gotama, so that both might have been equally well applied to any other person in India, if he had only excited the same feelings. The one ideal was chiefly due to political experiences, the other to philosophical speculations; the one was the ideal of a King of Righteousness, the other of an all-perfect Wisdom.

Just at the time when the early Buddhist literature regarding Gotama was reaching its canonical form, and the ideas of the Buddhists regarding him were being developed into what are now the orthodox views, the ancient political framework of Indian society was undergoing an inevitable and important change. The older division into clans, some of them patriarchal, some of them aristocratic republics, was passing into the more modern division into nations. A new power had arisen, and was making itself very clearly felt—the power of an autocratic king. At the end of the fourth century B.C., there had already been dynasties of kings in the two most powerful countries on the banks of the Ganges, Kosala and Magadha. And we then hear of the first great sovereign—that Chandragutta who possibly met with Alexander; with whom certainly Alexander's successor, Seleukos Nikator, first fought and then entered into treaty; and whose power extended from the eastern Ganges to beyond the Panjāb, and from the Himālaya mountains down to the Vindhya range. His victories and his far-reaching dominion brought home to the people the idea of a universal monarch.

They combined with this idea a theory, common to all progressive peoples in ancient times, incorporated into almost all the ancient religions, and derived from a very natural dissatisfaction with existing affairs—that theory of a golden age which men used to think must certainly have existed in the past, and which the modern belief, based on more accurate knowledge, places, with equal certitude, in the future. The ideal monarch, the Chakka-vatti, was a king of kings, irresistible and mighty, who ruled in righteousness over a happy people. He is often described in the Buddhist Suttas as "a king of kings, a righteous man who ruled in "righteousness, lord of the four quarters of the earth, "invincible, the protector of his people, possessor of "the seven royal treasures." The details of these royal treasures, and of four wonderful gifts, often associated with them as distinguishing marks of a king of kings, are particularly interesting as being compounded of the ancient and half-forgotten poetry of the sun-myth, and of the new and powerful ethics of Buddhism. When the stories told of the old gods, of the external spirits supposed to animate the powers of nature, and especially of the sun-god in his battles with the storm, had become misunderstood, the heroes of these stories were taken to be men, half human, half divine, and the glorious attributes ascribed to them were naturally applied and adapted to the new ideal.

The first of these treasures was the treasure of the Wheel, with its nave, its tire, and all its thousand spokes complete, which appears to the great king, when he has purified himself, and has gone up into the upper storey of his palace to keep the sacred day. The wheel is taken from the Vedic poetry, in which the sun had been described as rolling on in his victorious course across the space of heaven. And like the sun, when the wondrous wheel appears to the great king, it rolls onwards to the very extremities of the world conquering and to conquer. But the wheel of the ancient sun-worship is now subordinated to the king who has purified himself. It only subjugates the other kings it meets with to subject them to the righteous monarch, who lays down the sacred Buddhist laws: "Ye shall slay no living thing! Ye shall "not take what has not been given! Ye shall "not act wrongly touching the bodily desires! Ye "shall speak no lie! Ye shall drink no maddening "drink!" And in subjugating them, it brings the conquered ones under no lawless tyranny, for the ideal king then confirms his willing subjects in all their ancient privileges and rights.[1]

Secondly, the king of kings is the possessor of the wonderful White Elephant, which can carry its master across the broad earth to its very ocean boundary, and return home again in time for the morning meal. This is adapted from the mythical elephant Airāvata, "the Fertilizer," on which the sun-god Indra rides, the personification of the great, white, fertilizing rain-cloud, so rapid in its passage before the winds of the monsoon over the vault of heaven.[2]

Thirdly, the king of kings is the possessor of the Treasure of the Horse, "all white, with a black "head and a dark mane, wonderful in power, flying

---

[1] This is the full meaning of the yathābhuttaŋ bhuñjatha of the text Comp Rh. D., Buddhist Suttas from the Pāli, p 253.

[2] See Senart, Legende du Bouddha, pp 25—27, and Professor A. Kuhn, Herabkunft des Feuers, p 241.

"through the sky, the charger-king whose name was "Thunder-Cloud." The description is sufficient evidence of this figure being also derived from the ancient mythology, and from a part of it which has survived down to our own times, through the influence of the Greeks, in the horses of the sun. And it is easy to understand why the Western nations preserved this image of the ancient cloud-poetry rather than the last.

Fourthly, the king of kings is the possessor of a wondrous Gem, called the Veluriya, from which our word beryl is probably derived, "bright, of the "purest species, with eight facets, excellently wrought, "clear, transparent, perfect in every way."

That the gem was included among the royal treasures need not surprise us, and would seem to be explicable without any reference to the Vedic poetry. But when we find that "the splendour of that wondrous gem "spread round about a league on every side," and that "when the great king of glory, to test that wondrous "gem, set all his four-fold army in array, and raised "aloft the gem upon his standard-top, he was able to "march out in the gloom and darkness of the night, "and all the dwellers round about began their daily "work, thinking, 'The daylight hath appeared!'" we see that we have to do with no ordinary jewel. And when we recollect that the lightning with which Indra, in the hymns, slays the demon of the darkness, is called his jewel, and that mystical gems have survived in the later popular beliefs as gifted with supernatural powers, able to carry their happy possessors through the sky, or obtain for them prosperity and wealth, we see that here also we have a reminiscence of the poetry and mysticism of that Animism which is so hard to kill.

Fifthly, the king of kings is the possessor of a Pearl among Women, "graceful in figure, lovely "in appearance, charming in manner, and beautiful "in complexion; surpassing human beauty, she had "attained unto the beauty of the gods!" The two last treasures are a Treasurer and an Adviser, faithful servants, like the Pearl among women, of the king of kings. These are not apparently or necessarily adopted from the Vedic hymns, and the descriptions of them contain no details of peculiar interest: we can therefore pass on to the four Iddhis or wonderful gifts with which he is said to have been endowed.

These are simply such qualities of body and mind as would naturally be ascribed to the ideal king. He is, in the first place, "graceful in figure, handsome in "appearance, and pleasing in manner, beyond what "other men are." Secondly, he was "of long life, and "of many years, beyond those of other men." Thirdly, he was "free from disease, and from bodily suffering, "beyond what other men are." And fourthly, he was "beloved and popular with Brāhmans and with laymen "alike." As a father is near and dear to his sons, so is he said to have been to them; and as sons are near and dear to their father, so were they to him. Once, it is related, he was proceeding in royal pomp to his pleasure-ground. The people besought him, saying, "O "king, pass slowly by, that we may look upon thee for "a longer time!" But he, addressing his charioteer, replies, "Drive on the chariot slowly, charioteer, that "I may look upon my people for a longer time!" Such is the courtesy and such the mutual love which reigns in the golden age between the monarch and the people of his realm. Such is the Buddhist picture of the ideal king.

We shall be able better to enter into the feelings which prompted the early Buddhists in their application of this ideal to Gotama, if we call to mind the manner in which the Jewish ideal of a Messiah influenced the minds of the early Christians. The two ideals are of course not the same in detail, for they grew out of very different experiences, and were clothed in words drawn from very different literatures. But they are so remarkably similar, both in the sources, political and spiritual, from which they sprung, and in their most essential features, that the comparison of the two cannot fail to be historically instructive.

In the first place, just as the Messiah whom the Hebrews expected was very unlike him to whom the word was afterwards applied, so the Cakka-vatti was very unlike what Gotama really was The ideals existed before their supposed fulfilment; and they were only fulfilled by being put to a use so unthought of by those who held them, that they really ceased, as ideals, to exist. The Christian Messiah is as much higher and more noble than the previous conception of the first-century Jews, as the Buddhist King of Righteousness is higher and more noble than the previous Hindū conception of the King of Kings.

One may be allowed to say this without being supposed to detract from the great beauty of those earlier conceptions. We cannot but sympathize with that natural longing—to which Carlyle gave such varied and energetic expression—for the great man whose strong hand shall cut the gordian knot of the complicated difficulties of life, and shall set all things straight. And when we find that peoples so distant and so different as the Jews and the Indian Āryans, when imagining what kind of man such a man must be, built up such grand and glorious fancies as those of the Messiah and the Cakka-vatti, it can only strengthen our faith in humanity. But it was surely a truer instinct which guided the early Christians and the early Buddhists, when the eyes of their minds had been opened by the new teaching, to put the Teacher in the place of the King, and to look for the ideal kingdom in a kingdom of righteousness in the hearts of men. It was a change greater even, perhaps, than they really saw; for it made the motive-power, the strength, the hope of the new kingdom, to lie in the change of character in the individuals. It logically replaced the vain craving after a *deus ex machinā* in the guise of a benevolent despot, by the sure and certain hope of a wise philanthropy in the gradual elevation of mankind.

But the Buddhists, at least, had no such foresight as to draw this logical conclusion; they had only the insight to recognize in their Master the true Cakka-vatti. And when seeking for words and images in which to express their awe and love to him, they allowed the ideal of the Cakka-vatti to influence them in two ways. They used it, in the first place, as a type to which their descriptions of the Master, as their King of Righteousness, should conform. His chief disciple, Sāriputta, became known as the Prime Minister in that kingdom, and the Arahats were the body-guard of the king, who gave them the Sīlas (the lower morality described in the second Lecture) as a cloak, earnest meditation as a breastplate, continual mindfulness as a shield, patience as a staff, the Dhamma or true doctrine as a sword that overcomes all things incompatible with the Sīlas, and the insight of Arahatship as a gem to adorn their helmet. It was a battle they had to fight, a victory they had to win, under a Leader who himself had gone on in front to show the way. The rain-cloud, which was the appanage of the Cakka-vatti, rained down in the new teaching the ambrosia (Amata) of Arahatship, the fertilizer of all right desires, the extinguisher of the fatal fires of lust, of hatred, and of ignorance. And the mystic wheel became the wheel of the Dhamma, which the King of Righteousness himself had set rolling onwards in the first discourse he uttered—that supreme wheel of the empire of truth which not by any Samana or Brāhman, not by any god, not by any Brahmā or Māra, not by any being in the universe, can ever be turned back. Invincibly shall it roll onwards to the very boundaries of the world, until all the kings of the earth shall have become willing subjects of the mild empire of its lord, obedient followers of the law of truth!

It is an instructive instance of the way in which spiritual figures of speech harden and crystallize, in ignorant minds, into erroneous beliefs and baneful superstitions, that this beautiful parable, the only "turning of the wheel of the Dhamma" which we hear of in early Buddhism, has given rise to the use of the well-known praying-wheels—those curious machines which, filled with endless repetitions of a form of sacred words (themselves unknown in the earlier teaching), stand in the towns in every open place, are put up beside the foot-paths and the roads, and even, by the help of sails like those of windmills, are turned by every breeze which blows over the thrice sacred realm of the pope-king of the valleys of Tibet.

But, secondly—and here the early Buddhists were not so wise—they allowed their ideal of the Cakkavatti to influence their beliefs as to the actual facts of the outward conditions of Gotama's life. The petty chief, his father, became a powerful monarch of wide-spread dominions, though the geographical details of the legend really show to the slightest criticism how limited was the extent of the Sākya clan over whom he held only a modified chieftainship. The modest dwelling in which Gotama was born becomes a palace. The literature of somewhat later times provides him on his marriage with three palaces, one for use in each of the three seasons of the year. And he is supposed to have been brought up amidst every dignity and luxury which the minds of the Buddhist poets can conceive.

There are unmistakable traces in many of these details—into which I have no time to enter, and which vary in every book, growing in magnificence as the interval of time grows greater—of the ancient glory of the sun-god. And they also seem to me to afford undeniable evidence of a desire in the relators of these legends to express—in the same spirit as has inspired many Christian writers—the greatness of Gotama's renunciation. This is the motive which leads them to raise to the highest pitch the glories of the position he abandoned, when he is related to have left his father's throne, to which he, the only son, was heir; to have left his young wife and his only child behind him; to have left his bright home, with all its glories and delights, and to have gone out into the darkness of the night, to become a despised mendicant, and a lonely, homeless wanderer. The gorgeous descriptions of what he had resigned are indications, not only of the sources of Buddhist poetry, but also of the fact that the deepest impression he made upon his disciples was the lesson of self-renunciation, that Selbst-todtung, annihilation of self, which, according to one of our latest prophets, "is justly reckoned the beginning of all virtue."[1]

There is a modern poem by an English writer—Mr. Edwin Arnold's *Light of Asia*—which has caught very successfully, as it seems to me, the tone and spirit of the later forms of this side of the Cakka-vatti legends, and has given expression in eloquent words to the thoughts that stirred the hearts of the Buddhists of those times. And when we call to mind the process through which it has become possible for a Christian poet to sing of the carpenter's Son,

> "His Father's home of light,
> His rainbow-circled throne,
> He left for earthly night,
> For wanderings sad and lone,"[2]

we shall be able to read between the lines of these Buddhist Cakka-vatti legends, and to recognize in them, not merely empty falsehoods, the offspring of folly or

---

[1] Carlyle, *Jesuitism*, p 257.

[2] Hymns, Ancient and Modern, 239.

of fraud, but the only embodiment possible, under those conditions, of some of the noblest feelings that have ever moved the world.

---

Besides the ideal king, the personification of Power and Justice, another ideal has played an important part in the formation of early Buddhist ideas regarding their Master. This ideal, too, owed its birth at least to reminiscences of Vedic thought; but I venture to think, though the question is as yet beset with difficulties, that it had its principal developement during the later times in which the Buddhist Suttas were gradually assuming their present shape. It was the ideal of a perfectly Wise Man, the personification of Wisdom, the Buddha.

It had been held by the pre-Buddhistic Āryans in India that holy men, by properly performed ritual, by suitable sacrifice, could, in fact, compel the gods to yield to their irresistible influence; and that a life of self-denial and penance, joined with mysterious wisdom, would give to men superhuman power. The belief in transmigration, that the efficacy of deeds done in one life would be carried over to the next, gave to this idea additional force; while among the early Buddhists it received further confirmation from the supreme importance attached by Gotama to self-renunciation, to intellectual self-culture, and to wisdom.

There thus sprung up this ideal of the Buddha, the man who, through countless ages of heroic struggle in many different births, had at last attained to such perfect purity and perfect wisdom, that he was able, when goodness was dying out on earth, and men had become more and more wicked and depraved, to extinguish by his teaching the fires of their passion, to lead them along the way of escape from the net of transmigration, and thus in that evil time to save a lost world from impending ruin.

It was perhaps the memory of the great sages of old, the Rishis of the older teaching, that led the early Buddhists, if not Gotama himself, to believe that there had been previous Buddhas before Gotama. At first this belief was perhaps confined to the seven Buddhas (seven, that is, including Gotama himself), of whom separate mention is made in several of the Suttas. But already in some of the latest books included in the Pāli Piṭakas we hear of twenty-seven Buddhas, and in later times the number of these previous Buddhas was believed to be innumerable. And in the latest phases of the doctrine, as held in Nepāl and in Tibet, this world was held to have come into being through a series or chain of emanations, in which these previous Buddhas form the connecting links.

There is a great deal in these later emanations which

remind us of the Emanations of the Gnostic Christians; and the ideal of the Buddha has, even in early Buddhism, an influence similar, in many respects, to that of the Logos in early Christianity. But the divine element in the Gnostic theory distinguishes it from the Buddhist ideal Wisdom, just as the divine and solar elements in the Buddhist ideal king distinguish him from the ideal Messiah of the later pre-Christian Jews.

It was Gotama himself, in all probability, who gave the start to this latter phase of the new Buddhist conceptions, by his own belief, as recorded in the Suttas, that he was himself a Buddha. It is true that the writings of the early Buddhists are open to most suspicion precisely where they speak of the person of the Buddha. The doctrines of Buddhism are so original, and so far beyond the capacity of the early Buddhists, it is so very probable that before the end of his long career Gotama himself had completely worked out and enunciated them, that we may rely with less doubt upon the records of the Buddhist ethical system, than upon what the early Buddhists, profoundly influenced by the feelings to which reference has just been made, have said about their revered Master himself But the belief in his own Buddhahood is placed, in the very oldest parts of the Pitakas, so often in Gotama's mouth, and at such important crises in his career, that it is hard not to believe that the tradition is, in this respect, correct. And it receives also what seems to me to be a very real support from the unquestioned facts that other teachers under similar conditions have held similar beliefs regarding themselves.

Thus, after the close of that greatest of all events in his life, his long struggle and final victory over Māra, the Evil One, in the jungle, and the subsequent long fast of four times seven days, Gotama is said to have announced his Buddhahood to the first person whom he meets. He was then on his way to Benāres to publish the good news of the truth he had just found to his five friends, the Pañcavaggiya ascetics. The account in the Pāli Introduction to the Book of Buddhist Birth Stories goes on:

"The five ascetics, seeing already from afar the "Buddha coming, said one to another, 'Friend! here "'comes the Samaṇa Gotama. He has turned aside "'again to the free use of the necessaries of life, and "'has recovered roundness of form, acuteness of sense, "'and beauty of complexion. We ought to pay him "'no reverence; but as he is, after all, of a good "'family, he deserves the honour of a seat. So we "'will simply prepare a seat for him.'

"Then the Blessed One, casting about in his mind "(by the power that he had of knowing what was "going on in the thoughts of all beings) as to what "they were thinking of, knew their thoughts. And "concentrating that feeling of his love which was able "to pervade generally all beings in earth and heaven, "he directed it specially towards them. So the sense "of his love diffused itself through their hearts. And "as he came nearer and nearer, unable any longer to "adhere to their resolve, they arose from their seats, "and bowed down before him, and welcomed him with "every demonstration of respect. But not knowing "that he had become a Buddha, they addressed him, "in everything they said, either by name or as 'Good "'friend!' Then the Blessed One announced to them "his Buddhahood, saying: 'O Samanas, address not "'a Buddha by his name or as Good friend! And I, "'O Samanas, am become a Buddha, as those who "'have gone before!'"[1]

The expression used here in the oldest account of this meeting known to me (that in the first Khandhaka)[2] is Arahaŋ Sammā-sambuddho, words very familiar to all who read native Buddhist books, as they are repeated on the opening page of each treatise. They seem to me to be perfectly simple in meaning, and not to hide any mystery at all Arahaŋ is an Arahat, one who has reached the end of Gotama's so-called Noble Path, and is free from the fatal dispositions of mind to sensuality, individuality, delusion and ignorance. Sammā is perfect, complete in all its parts; and Sambuddha is merely, as we should say, "a "very Buddha."

---

[1] Buddhist Birth Stories, p 112.

[2] Mahāvagga, i 6, 12

There were, namely, two kinds of Buddhas or men of insight; firstly, those who have seen through things, and being free from delusions (more especially the delusions of Animistic views on the one hand, and of worldliness on the other) are completely, so to speak, out of the jungle, and in the open. But they cannot trace back the several parts of the path by which they have themselves escaped, so as to be able to guide others along it. They are Pacceka-Buddhas, that is, "enlightened only for one." Quite emancipated themselves, they are like a revelation in some unknown tongue, from which others can receive no immediate deliverance; or, to take a modern instance, like one who holds perfectly sound views of science or of history, and never therefore talks heresy, but through want of enthusiasm, absence of the power of exposition, moral timidity, or fear of being detected in a fault, observes so discreet a silence that his knowledge dies with him. Only at rare intervals, once and again in hundreds of ages, does "a very Buddha," one who has the insight and can also make others see, appear in the world, and happy are they who meet him. As was said in the passage I read last Tuesday week from the Tevijja Sutta, he not only himself "understands and "sees as it were face to face," but "he makes his "knowledge known to others. He proclaims the "Dhamma, the Truth, both in its letter and in its "spirit; he makes known the higher life in all its "purity and in all its perfectness."

All this is of peculiar interest from the comparative point of view. It is an expression from the Buddhist standpoint, which excludes the theory of a Supreme Deity, of an idea very similar to that which is expressed in Christian writings when Christ is represented as the manifestation of God to men, the Logos, the Word of God made flesh, the Bread of Life. And it is not a mere chance that heterodox followers of the two religions have afterwards used the Buddha and the Logos conceptions as bases of their emanation theories. It is only a fresh instance of the way in which similar ideas in similarly constituted minds come to be modified in very similar ways.

The Cakka-vatti Buddha was to the early Buddhists what the Messiah Logos was to the early Christians. In both cases the two ideas overlap one another, run into one another, supplement one another. In both cases the two combined cover as nearly the same ground as the different foundations of the two teachings will permit. And it is the Cakka-vatti Buddha circle of ideas in the one case, just as the Messiah Logos in the other, that has had the principal influence in determining the opinions of the early disciples as to the person of their Master. The method followed in the early Buddhist and early Christian biographies of their respective Masters was the same, and led to similar results; though the details are in no particular quite identical in the two cases.

Before venturing to suggest what seems to me to be the only obvious conclusion to be drawn from this parallel, I would add that besides these two ideals of Power and Wisdom, the reverse of discreditable to those who formed and held them, other influences were by no means without weight in the formation of the Buddhist lives of Gotama. It is a universal tendency, exemplified not only in ancient lives of popular saints and of popular heroes, but in modern every-day life, to discover in the childhood of men who have afterwards become eminent or famous, clear prognostications of their future greatness. As these discoveries are made after the event, they are often apposite enough; and in the case of the King of Righteousness, they took the shape that he descended of his own accord into his mother's womb from his throne in heaven; that at his birth heaven and earth united to pay him homage; while the angels sang their songs of victory, and archangels were present with their help. His mother was the best and purest of the daughters of men, and had no other son; and his conception took place without the aid of his father. His mother has dreams of his future greatness; and there are prophecies at his birth that her son will become either a Cakka-vatti or a Buddha, who will remove the veils of ignorance and sin from the world. In his youth he excels all his companions, and even teaches the teachers who were appointed to instruct him; while aged saints unite to pay him honour, and sing hymns to his praise.

All these details were doubtless purely imaginary. But they were not due to one mind; they were the work of time, and no one who bore a part in their creation was consciously manufacturing untruth. The early biographers did not sufficiently distinguish between what they thought ought to have happened and what did really happen, between that which seemed edifying to them and that which was true in fact. But I cannot believe that they ever set to work deliberately to forge any part of their narrative.

And this brings us to a fourth cause to which much that is legendary is due. Their natural belief that the miraculous was probable, their abiding faith in the constant presence of supernatural beings, in the constant action of supernatural causes, led the early Buddhists easily to see what they so fully expected to find. The struggles of Gotama's mind become the temptations of Māra, the spirit of Evil; his moments of exaltation are ascribed to the visits of angels; his thoughts of resolution or of triumph become songs in angel mouths; and a few circumstances, explicable even now as natural, are related as miraculous events.

A few details, but these are later, are due to yet another cause. There were local relics to be sanctified, local legends to receive authority from the sacred story. The Ceylonese claim to possess one of Gotama's teeth and the bones of his neck. They consequently believe and relate an episode in his life explaining how these relics were obtained.[1] The Burmese have another tooth and another strange story to support it.[2] But none of these stories are to be found in the Pitaka account of the Buddha's death, which is indeed inconsistent with them all.[3] And in a similar way stories not found in the earliest authorities occur in the later books, according to which images then existing had been actually made in the very lifetime of the Teacher.[4]

Finally, when all the incredible details due to the different causes just referred to have been deducted, there remain a certain number of miraculous incidents which are apparently due to the mere love of the marvellous, the origin of which cannot at present be ascribed to any more definite source than the depraved and weak imagination of the narrators, who did not perceive that these stories, so far from heightening, really veiled and lowered their idea of Gotama, and were irreconcilable with the real facts of his life.

---

[1] Dāthāvaṃsa, ii. 51, 52

[2] Bigandet, Legend of the Burmese Buddha, p 343.

[3] Mahā-parinibbāna Sutta, vi 35—62

[4] Koppen, Geschichte des Buddhismus, i. 99, ii. 63, 102.

There now arises the very natural question, whether all this is any proof that the Christian writers, who lived about five hundred years after the Buddhist writers, borrowed their ideas from India? The resemblances are so very striking, that this question has often been unhesitatingly answered in the affirmative; but more often, I think, in popular lectures and in magazine articles than in independent books, and more often by those who are glad to throw discredit on Christianity than by serious scholars. The fullest treatment of it from this last point of view is, however, in a very learned work by a writer of thoroughly earnest and unbiassed mind, I mean the Angel Messiah of Buddhists, Essenes and Christians, by Mr. Ernest de Bunsen. The curious reader will find in this volume a very exhaustive statement of all the possible channels through which such a borrowing by the Christians from the Buddhists can be supposed to have taken place. There is neither time nor space at the close of this Lecture to enter upon the long and varied argument which is there set forth. I will only say that I have carefully considered it throughout with a mind quite open to conviction, and that I can find no evidence whatever of any actual and direct communication of any of these ideas from the East to the West. Where the Gospel narratives resemble the Buddhist ones, they seem to me to have been independently developed on the shores of the Mediterranean and in the valley of the Ganges; and strikingly similar as they often are at first sight, the slightest comparison is sufficient to show that they rested throughout on a basis of doctrine fundamentally opposed.

If this view be correct, it remains therefore that the similarities of idea are evidence not of any borrowing from the one side or the other, but of similar feelings engendered in men's minds by similar experiences; an explanation which fully accounts not only for all the similarities, but also for all the differences. And when it is considered that only twice in the history of the world have all the circumstances combined to render the origin of such ideas possible, it must be acknowledged that the lessons drawn from the study of early Buddhism may be found as useful for the true appreciation of early Christianity as the Vedas are useful for the true appreciation of classical mythology. Or, in other words, that those who are willing to discuss both religions on the same principles may expect to find, in the history of early Buddhism, not only an historical example by which they may test their methods of investigation, but an historical parallel from which they may condescend to learn.

## LECTURE V

# GOTAMA'S ORDER.

---

Among the points of Buddhist history most instructive from a comparative point of view, there is probably none more important than the fate of Gotama's Saṅgha, the Community or Society of those who had given up the world to carry out the new ideas. For, as in the case of his ethical system, so also in the practical organization of this body of his more earnest and devoted adherents, he made use of already existing ideas and customs.

The valley of the Ganges in the sixth century before the Christian era was a land which did not contain a single book or a single church. There were no preachers in it, no editors, nothing like what we should call a university. There were the Brāhman schools of ritual; and, as part of the ritual was the repetition of sacred words, grammar and recitation were taught there as accessories to correct learning by heart and accurate repetition. And in these schools codes of ancient customs were handed down by word of mouth.

But those who had some thoughts of their own to propound, something to say apart from tradition, were in the habit of gathering disciples round them in the same way as was done in Greece by the philosophers, at a time when things had there reached a corresponding point in the parallel developements of these two communities. There seem to have been not a few of such self-elected teachers. They led for the most part very simple lives; depending for their subsistence on the voluntary offerings of the multitude (always ready and even eager to worship). And while there was no little sophistry, and a good deal of jugglery, mental and manual, practised among them, there were also in their ranks not a few really earnest and by no means altogether unsuccessful inquirers. It is worth notice in passing that several of these sophists were women (though there are traces of the disfavour with which the severer spirits, even in far-off times, looked upon that phase of the movement), and that the majority of them belonged to one or other of the lower castes. They had of course not the faintest suspicion of scientific or historical methods of inquiry. They fully believed they could stretch straight out and grasp the ultimate truth, like children reaching forth to seize the moon—a hope that has not yet faded away, as we see from the case of those among us now who argue, as it were, from their own hearth-rugs upwards. And being unacquainted with any language save their own, conclusions about words seemed to them as real as conclusions about things. It was no unusual thing for them to wander from place to place ready to maintain theses against all the world. And there was great public interest in such tournaments, which it was the custom to terminate by the vanquished acknowledging the victor as his master, and entering the ranks of his disciples.

We have grown out of such things since the days of Luther; and the confusion of tongues has helped us to understand that we cannot build a tower up to heaven by laying words on words. We have something of the insight of humility; and, aiming not so high, are beginning to make a surer progress by steps that can never be thrown down. Gotama went as far as was possible in those times in the same direction. He looked at all the systems as Hume looked at the philosophies; and the Buddhist Suttas seem never tired of representing him as inveighing against diṭṭhi, literally View, and its "viewy" or "crotchety" professors

But the real analogue to Gotama, as we should naturally expect, is a man of very different character from David Hume, and of much less modern mind. In his place in history, in his methods of exposition, in many of his personal qualities, Gotama stands side by side with Socrates: and it is strange that the comparison has never been thus pointed out before. But in one most important particular he was much more than Socrates. He had a completely elaborated scheme of practical life, a carefully thought-out system of inward self-culture, to put in the place of the systems of philosophy on the one hand, and those of ritual on the other. It was the desire to carry out this system into practice that led to the establishment of his Society, and that imposed upon it its peculiar character.

It was at first, no doubt, simply a body of disciples. Like the other teachers, Gotama and his followers lived on alms; like them, they adopted a peculiar dress; like them, they sought for converts; and, as in other such bodies, their numbers were constantly changing, individuals joining or leaving the general body as they felt disposed. A slight difference brought about the first important change. In the case of other teachers, the disciples were dependent on the presence of the Master; and there being no appeal to the masses, the number of disciples was kept within moderate limits. The success of Buddhism in its earliest years has doubtless been somewhat exaggerated in the Pāli Suttas. But when we recollect that Gotama's system of self-training was one which all were invited to adopt, and which could be carried out irrespective of residence at any particular spot or in any particular company, we can easily understand how it came to pass that the disciples were not confined only to those who could remain with the Master. Either during his visits, or at other times, these isolated followers would receive fresh adherents; and it was in consequence of the number of such accessions, according to the Khandakas, that permission came to be granted to Gotama's disciples to receive fresh disciples into the Society without consulting or referring the matter to him. From that moment the existence of the Society was assured, even after its founder had passed away. The body of personal followers had become an Order—the oldest, as it is the most numerous and the most influential, of all the numerous Orders of religious brethren which the world has seen.

In order at all to understand either Buddhism itself or the significance of the history of Buddhism, we must endeavour, however difficult the task may be, to enter into the feelings of those who were induced thus to give up everything in order to devote themselves to a mode of life which Englishmen as a rule regard with something approaching very nearly to contempt. I would not quarrel with that feeling. What we shall have to set forth in this Lecture will show, indeed, how great is its excuse, or perhaps even its justification; and it no doubt depends in reality upon what is the surest basis for correct judgment on such questions, upon the lessons of history. I would only protest against what seems to me to be the abuse of it—a closing of one's eyes to what can be said on the other side, the attaching of an exaggerated importance to those things which the recluse, perhaps rightly, looks down upon as worse than worthless.

In Gotama's time the experiment had not as yet been fully tried, and we can scarcely wonder that its dangers had not been foreseen. There is a dissatisfaction attached to the pursuit of wealth, there is an unreality in social success, there are sorrows inseparably involved in family life, that must strike the most careless observer, and that soon impress themselves upon those who do not observe, but only experience. There are problems in life that baffle the acutest inquiry; and when the turn of affairs has brought these problems to the front, without offering any other solution, it is not unnatural to men to suppose that at least an escape from them can be found in the quiet life of the cloister, where peace and calmness reign.

It is this longing after peace that gives us the clue to the strange fact that hundreds and thousands, in Buddhist and in Christian countries, have given up all things else that men live and long for, counting them but as dross. So we are told in the Khandhakas that when the people were astonished that the great and famous Brāhman, Kassapa of Uruvelā, had left all to join the new Teacher, and the latter asks him to explain it, saying:

"What hast thou seen, O thou of Uruvelā,
That thou, for penances so far renowned,
Forsakest thus thy sacrificial fire?
I ask thee, Kassapa, the meaning of this thing:
. How comes it that thine altar lies deserted?"

He answers:

"'Tis of such things as sights, and sounds, and tastes,
Of women, and of lusts, the ritual speaks.
When these I saw to be the dregs of life,
I felt no charm in offerings small or great."

Gotama rojoins:

"But if thy mind no longer finds delight
In sights and sounds, and things that please the taste,
What is it, in the world of men or gods,
That thy heart longs for? Tell me that, Kassapa!"

And the convert answers:

"That state of Peace I saw, wherein the roots
Of new existences are all destroyed; and greed,
And hatred, and delusion, all have ceased,—
The state from lust of future life set free;
That changeth not, can ne'er be led to change.
My mind saw that! What care I for those rites?"[1]

It is this same longing for peace which is represented

---

[1] The first Khandhaka, chap xxii § 5. Compare Buddhist Birth Stories, pp 114, 115

to have been the deciding motive which led Gotama himself to abandon the world. The last authority quoted says of him also:

"The Bodisat, riding in his splendid chariot, entered "the town with great magnificence and exceeding "glory. At that time a noble virgin, Kisā Gotamī by "name, had gone to the flat roof of the upper storey of "her palace, and she beheld the beauty and majesty "of the Bodisat as he was proceeding through the city. "Pleased and delighted at the sight, she burst forth "into this song of joy:

"Blessed indeed is that mother,—
Blessed indeed is that father,—
Blessed indeed is that wife,—
Who owns this Lord so glorious!

"Hearing this, the Bodisat thought to himself, 'On "'catching sight of such a one the heart of his mother "'is made happy, the heart of his father is made "'happy, the heart of his wife is made happy! This "'is all she says. But by what can every heart attain "'to lasting happiness and peace?' And to him whose "mind was estranged from sin the answer came, 'When "'the fire of lust is gone out, then peace is gained; "'when the fires of hatred and delusion are gone out, "'then peace is gained; when the troubles of mind, "'arising from pride, credulity, and all other sins, have "'ceased, then peace is gained! Sweet is the lesson "'this singer makes me hear, for the Nirvāna of Peace "'is that which I have been trying to find out. This "'very day I will break away from household cares! "'I will renounce the world! I will follow only after "'the Nirvāna itself!'"[1]

This immortal peace, this unchangeable state, to be reached here on this earth, this Nirvāna of Arahatship, was looked upon by the early Buddhists as better than all else that the world could bestow. It is the highest happiness, the bliss that passeth not away, in which even death hath lost its sting and the grave its victory, and all the difficulties and trials of life, its gains and ills, its hopes and its despair, have passed away for ever in a perfect Rest.

William Frederick Robertson's words will help us to understand this position, when he says, without a thought of Buddhism, "The deepest want of man is

[1] Buddhist Birth Stories, pp 79, 80. The force of this passage is due to the fulness of meaning which, to the Buddhist, the words Nibbuta and Nibbānaŋ convey. No words in Western languages cover exactly the same ground, or connote the same ideas To explain them fully to any one unfamiliar with Indian modes of thought would be difficult anywhere, and impossible in a note, but their meaning is pretty clear from the above sentences Where in them, in the song, the words blessed, happy, peace, and the words gone out, ceased, occur, Nibbuta stands in the original in one or other of its two meanings, where in them the words Nirvāna, Nirvāna of Peace, occur, Nibbānaŋ stands in the original Nirvāna is a lasting state of happiness and peace, to be reached here on earth by the extinction of the "fires" and "troubles" mentioned in this passage

"not a desire for happiness, but a craving for peace. "The real strength and majesty of the soul of man is "calmness, the manifestation of strength, the peace of "God ruling, the word of Christ saying to the inward "spirit, 'Peace,' and there is a great calm." And again: "Peace, then, is the opposite of passion; and of "labour, toil and trouble . . . . that state in which "there are no desires—in which there is no misery, no "remorse, no sting. And to this, says the Apostle, ye "are called—the grand peculiar call of Christianity— "the call, 'Come unto me, all ye that labour and are "'heavy laden, and I will give you—REST.'"

It was the distinguishing characteristic of Gotama, as the Buddha, that particular quality which made him to be a "very Buddha," that he had not only found this Rest for himself, but that he called others to partake of it; that he had the power to lead others to understand it, desire it, realize it. And though the state is a mental state, independent of outward conditions, though Nirvāna might be reached by those who had not abandoned the world, the Suttas of the early Buddhists are filled with the belief, doubtless shared, if not originated, by Gotama himself, that the attainment of it amidst the distractions of business or of family life was difficult in the extreme.

A very suggestive writer, full of the most modern spirit, speaks quite seriously of that "calmness and "serenity of soul which is unattainable by those "who still breathe the atmosphere of the domestic "hearth, and are liable to be swayed and perturbed by "the emotions inseparable from the love of the earthly, "the perishable, and the imperfect."[1] So we heard in the Tevijja Sutta the other day how, when he has listened to the words of the Buddha, the convert thinks: "Full of hindrances is household life, a path defiled "by passion: free as the air is the life of him who has "renounced all worldly things. How difficult is it for "the man who dwells at home to live the higher life "in all its fulness, in all its purity, in all its bright "perfection!"

And numberless other passages might be quoted from the Suttas in which the same idea is implied, though the opposition of the two conditions is not often so directly stated.

Thus, when we read: "The life which brings about "gain is one thing, but another is the life that leads "to Nirvāna. When the Bhikkhu, the disciple of the "Master, has perceived this, let him not take delight "in honour in the world, but let him seek rather after "separation from it:"[2]—we feel that the "separation "from it" means being so not only in mind, but also in actual life.

And again: "A wise man should leave the doctrine "of darkness, and follow the doctrine of light. Going

[1] Greg, Enigmas of Life, p 153.

[2] Dhammapadaŋ, verse 75.

"forth from his home into the homeless state, let "him, in retirement, seek there for joy where joy "seems difficult. Leaving all pleasures behind, and "free from hindrances, let the wise man purify himself "from all evil states of mind."[1]

In these verses the condemnation is clear, not only of the state of a man who is too much immersed in worldly cares, but also of the state of a man who is at all exposed to their distracting influence.

Here is another such passage:

"Let us live happily then, free from hatred among "the hating. Among men who hate, let us dwell "free from hatred!

"Let us live happily then, free from ailments among "the ailing. Among men who are sick at heart, let "us dwell free from affliction!

"Let us live happily then, free from care among the "careworn. Among men who are eager, let us dwell "free from eagerness!

"Let us live happily then, as those who have no "hindrances! We shall be like the bright gods who "feed on happiness!"[2]

Surely all this is really an outburst in praise of the state of those who had left the world, and had no cares and no hindrances because they had entered the

---

1 Dhammapadaŋ, verses 87, 88

2 Ibid. verses 197—200

## BUDDHIST IDOLS AND SYMBOLS.

1. Buddha. 2. The Trisul. 3. The Wheel. 4. The Lion.
5. The Tree, Umbrellas, and Garlands (Buddha Gaya). 6. Adi-Buddha.

*Didarganj: Chowry Bearer,*
*1st. Century A.D.*

*Bodhisattva from Kanheri*

*Gandhara: Standing Bodhisattva. 2nd or 3rd century A.D.*

*Standing Buddha; Chaitya Slab: Nagarjunakonda*
*(Photo: by courtesy of P. Ramachandra Rao.)*

*Bodhisattva Avalokitesvara: Sarnath, 5th century A.D.*

*Buddha: Bronze, from Sultanganj, 5th century A.D*

*A Brahmin or Bhikshu. Excellent drawing, combining "Significant form" line rhythm and simple decorative colour pattern. The type of Gupta art which influenced the China of the T'ang Dynasty; its ideals have been preserved in Japan up to the colour woodcuts of the 18th and 19th centuries and have again influenced modern western art. Middle of 5th century A.D. Cave VI.*

Society of Gotama's disciples. So it is clearly of life in the Order that the beautiful lines are spoken:

"When the wise man by earnestness has driven
Vanity far away, the terraced heights
Of wisdom doth he climb, and, free from care,
Looks down on the vain world, the careworn
crowd—
As he who stands upon a mountain-top
Looks down, serene, on toilers in the plains."

It is possible, no doubt, to object that it is the inward state which is here referred to, and that we have nothing more than the feeling expressed at greater length in the well-known lines of Lucretius, where he says:

"It may be sweet when on the great sea the winds "trouble its waters to behold from land another's deep "distress; not that it is a pleasure and delight that "any should be afflicted, but because it is sweet to see "from what evils you are yourself exempt. It may be "sweet also to look upon the mighty struggles of war "arrayed along the plains without sharing yourself in "the danger But nothing is more sweet than to hold "the lofty and serene positions, well fortified by the "learning of the wise, from which you may look down "upon others, and see them wandering all abroad, and "going astray in their search for the path of life; see "the contest among them of intellect, of rivalry, of "birth, the striving night and day with surpassing "effort to struggle up to the summit of power, and be "masters of the world. O miserable minds of men! "O blinded breasts! in what darkness of life and in "how great dangers is passed all this term of life, "whatever its duration! Why will you not see that "nature craves for itself nothing more than that the "man from whose body pain holds aloof, should in "mind enjoy a feeling of pleasure, exempt from care "and fear?"[1]

This analogy was already pointed out by Mr. Childers, in whom we lost not only a scholar of quite unusual promise, but also one whose real sympathy with the deeper side of early Buddhism enabled him to throw an unexpected light on many dark and difficult passages in their sacred writings. But he would have been the first to maintain that the allusion of the Buddhist lines is not only to Nirvāna, but also to life in the Order. Readers of Thomas à Kempis will find it by no means difficult to understand the tone of mind which, fully recognizing the possibility of goodness to those who live in the world, still looks upon the state of those who have left it as the proper and natural aim of those who are earnestly bent upon the attainment of the highest forms of the religious life.

It is the constant repetition of the allusion to such

---

[1] Lucretius, Book ii ad. init "Suave mari magno," &c I follow Mr Munro's version.

a view of life in similar passages, which leads us to the undoubting conclusion that a spirit of renunciation of the world really filled the minds both of Gotama himself and of his first disciples, and even to the suspicion that this feeling was very prevalent in early Buddhist times, and prepared the hearts of those who listened to early Buddhist teaching The idea was in the air; men were already favourably inclined towards it; and the new movement contributed to it the energetic motive force of a strong emotion, and the guiding influence in the direction it should take.

I am quite aware that a cold criticism can point to clear and painful evidence of mental weakness, of personal rivalries, even of moral failings, in some of the early disciples; and it may ask how it was possible for such men to be moved by the kind of feelings suggested in the passages I have just quoted. I have the greatest respect for such criticism when it is dealing with points of literary history or of philological investigation. But it is much more likely to err on the negative than on the positive side when it attempts to pass judgment on the emotional, even fickle, movements of masses of men.

We have a curious instance of this in the case of one of the greatest scholars England has produced. When, at the first rise of monasticism in the basin of the Mediterranean, an enthusiasm for the solitary life, not unlike that which was prevalent in the times we are discussing in the valley of the Ganges, led men of all ranks and classes, and in incredible numbers, to devote themselves to a religious life in retirement from the haunts of men, this is the kind of explanation which Gibbon, paraphrasing the verses of a pagan litterateur, is pleased to give:

"The whole island is filled, or rather defiled, by men "who fly from the light. They call themselves monks, "or solitaries, because they choose to live alone, with- "out any witnesses of their actions. They fear the "gifts of fortune, from the apprehension of losing "them; and lest they should be miserable, they embrace "a life of voluntary wretchedness. How absurd is "their choice! how perverse their understanding! to "dread the evils, without being able to support the "blessings of the human condition! Either this melan- "choly madness is the effect of disease, or else the "consciousness of guilt urges these unhappy men to "exercise on their own bodies the tortures which are "inflicted on fugitive slaves by the hands of Justice."[1]

One is tempted to say, "How absurd is this judg- "ment! how perverse the understanding which can "see no motives but these in conduct so opposed to "the spirit of Vanity Fair!" The perhaps too eloquent pages of Montalembert tell a different tale; but there are witnesses enough among the Christian eremites themselves to show how inadequate and one-sided is such an estimate. Hear what Jerome says, himself

---

[1] Gibbon, c 29 (ed. Bohn, iii 328, 329) He is paraphrasing Claudii Rutilii De Reditu Suo, i. 439—448

one of them, when he invites his fellow-christians to join their ranks:

"O desert, blooming with the flowers of Christ! "O solitude, in which are found those stones of which "the city of the great King is built in the Apocalypse! "O loneliness, delighting in intercourse in God! What "do you, Brother, in secular life, who art greater "than the world? How long shall the shadows of "roofs oppress you? How long shall the prison-house "of smoky cities enclose you? Believe me, I know "not how much more light I gaze upon. It is well, "having cast off the burden of the body, to fly off to "the pure effulgence of the sky.

"Do you fear poverty? Christ calls the poor blessed. "Do you dread labour? No athlete is crowned without "sweat. Do you think of diet? Faith fears not "hunger. Do you fear to lay your body, wasted with "fasting, on the naked ground? The Lord will lie "down with you. Do you shrink from the undressed "hair of a neglected head? Your head is Christ. "Are you fearful of the boundless extent of the soli-"tude? You mentally walk in paradise. As often "as you ascend thither in contemplation, you will not "be in SOLITUDE."[1]

The critic may think such thoughts absurd, and the understanding that accepts them only perverse; but

---

[1] Jerome, Ep ad Heliodorum (Op ed. Erasm. i f 2)

we may venture to sympathize a little with them, so far, at least, as to enable us to follow the history of those strange men who thought them. It seems to me, I confess, that such as this was the tone, the spirit, that gave life to the monastic side of the early Buddhist movement, and that in this respect we must accept the evidence of the early Buddhist recluses themselves.

---

And I would go even further still. The passion for renunciation among the early Buddhists did not stand alone. It came comparatively earlier with them than it came in the history of the Christian Church, and it was strengthened and supported by other feelings, more like those which animated the very first disciples in New-Testament times. The history of Buddhism, when the Pāli Piṭakas were being formed, shows us the rise of monasticism coincident and combined with the glow of faith that distinguishes the rise of a new religion.

Chief among these is the strong attractive power of the personal character of the founder of the religion. When the Buddhist Society was being formed, Gotama was still living among them, and in daily contact with them, as their guide and master and example; and their love to him has tinged the Buddhist writings with a tone of personal affection and reverence that is occasionally very striking, and must have been a powerful factor in the young Society.

Thus we are told at the end of the Sutta Nipāta of an aged Brāhman going to Gotama with the plaintive appeal, "I am old, feeble, colourless! My eyes "are not clear, my hearing is not good! Lest I should "perish a fool on the way, tell me the Dhamma, that "I may know how here in this world to escape decay "and birth!"

Gotama sets forth the answer, in accordance with the doctrine of Arahatship, that he must give up longing for existence in any form, and must get rid of that craving thirst which would lead to such existence being renewed The aged Brāhman is convinced, the eyes of his mind are opened; he who was on the brink of death feels himself saved just at the time when hope was almost at an end. Bāvari, an old friend and fellow-Brāhman, then apparently asks him what has wrought the great change in him, for he is represented as replying to Bāvari:

"I will proclaim accordingly the way to the further "shore"—so said the venerable Pingiya. "As he saw "it, so he told it—he, the very wise, the passionless, "the desireless Lord. For why should he speak "falsely?"

But this reference to the teacher turns off the old man's thoughts even from the teaching, and he changes the subject of his speech:

"Well! I will praise that beautiful voice; the voice "of Him who is without stain and folly; who has left "arrogance and self-righteousness far behind!

"The darkness-dispelling Buddha, the all-seeing, "who understands all conditions, who has overcome all "existences, who is free from the passions, and has "put an end to pain—rightly is he called the Buddha "—he, O Brāhmana, hath come nigh even to me.

"And so, as a bird would pass the dense jungle by, "and take up his abode in the fruitful forest, even so "I, leaving the men of narrow views, am like a swan "who has gained the broad waters.

"Those who before explained to me the teaching of "Gotama, saying, 'Thus was it, thus it shall be,' all "that was only at secondhand, all that but added to "my doubts.

"There is only one living who can dispel the dark-"ness. That is the high-born, the luminous; Gotama "of great understanding, Gotama of great wisdom, who "taught me the truth, the instantaneous, immediate "destroyer of thirst, deliverance from distress—the "like whereof is nowhere!"

Then says Bāvari to him, "Canst thou then stay "away from him even for a moment, O Pingiya?"

And the old man rejoins:

"Not even for a moment do I stay away from him, "O Brāhmana. I see him in my mind and with my "eye, vigilant, O Brāhmana, night and day. In "reverencing him do I spend the night; therefore, "methinks, I am not far from him.

"Belief and joy, mind and thought, incline me "towards the doctrine of Gotama. Whichsoever way "the very wise man goes, that self-same way my "heart, too, turns

"I am worn out, and old, and feeble. 'Tis true, "therefore, my body cannot go. But in my thoughts "I always go there; for my heart, O Brāhmana, is "joined to him!"

And as Pingiya sat there, picturing to his friend his reverence for Gotama, and telling how he was not far from him, there shone round about them a golden light, and lo! a vision, sent forth by the Buddha himself, appeared before them. And Pingiya saw once more, and with his bodily eyes, the Blessed One standing, as it were, before him, and saying.

"As the faith of Vakkhali became set free from "doubt, and the faith of Bhadrāvudha grew clear, and "of Gotama of Ālavi, even so shalt thou, too, make "clear thy faith; thou shalt reach, O Pingiya, the "further shore (the haven that is outside) of the realm "of death."

It was perhaps only a perverse intelligence that could so exaggerate the insight and the wisdom of Gotama; it may be absurd to say that a vision of the Buddha could thus really and outwardly have appeared; the whole story may be a legend. But it must have been the hand of love that has penned a legend so touching and so beautiful, and which affords evidence—equally strong, whether it be poetic fancy, or a relation of what the writer thought to be actual fact—of the mighty influence of Gotama's personal character.

---

How the Great Teacher used that influence as regards the Society is set forth at the beginning of the Book of the Great Decease. It is there recorded that Gotama said to the assembled brethren:

"'I will teach you, O mendicants, seven conditions "'of the welfare of the Society. Listen well and "'attend, and I will speak.'

"'Even so, Lord,' said the brethren in assent to the "Blessed One; and he spake as follows:

"'So long, O mendicants, as the brethren meet "'together in full and frequent assemblies—so long "'as they meet together in concord, and rise in con- "'cord, and carry out in concord the duties of the "'order—so long as the brethren shall establish no- "'thing that has not been already prescribed, and "'abrogate nothing that has been already established, "'and act in accordance with the rules of the order as "'now laid down—so long as the brethren honour and "'esteem and revere and support the elders of expe- "'rience and long standing, the fathers and leaders of "'the order, and hold it a point of duty to hearken to "'their words—so long as the brethren fall not under "'the influence of that craving which, springing up "'within them, would give rise to renewed existence "'—so long as the brethren delight in a life of soli-"'tude—so long as the brethren so train their minds "'that good and holy men shall come to them, and "'those who have come shall dwell at ease—so long "'may the brethren be expected, not to decline, but "'to prosper. So long as these seven conditions shall "'continue to exist among the brethren, so long as "'they are well instructed in these conditions, so long "'may the brethren be expected not to decline, but to "'prosper.

"'Other seven conditions of welfare will I teach "'you, O brethren. Listen well and attend, and I "'will speak.'

"And on their expressing their assent, he spake as "follows:

"'So long as the brethren shall not engage in, or "'be fond of, or be connected with business—so long "'as the brethren shall not be in the habit of, or be "'fond of, or be partakers in idle talk—so long as the "'brethren shall not be addicted to, or be fond of, "'or indulge in slothfulness—so long as the brethren "'shall not frequent, or be fond of, or indulge in "'society—so long as the brethren shall neither have, "'nor fall under the influence of, sinful desires—so "'long as the brethren shall not become the friends, "'companions, or intimates of sinners—so long as the "'brethren shall not come to a stop on their way [to "'Nirvāna[1]] because they have attained to any lesser "'thing—so long may the brethren be expected not "'to decline, but to prosper.

"'So long as these conditions shall continue to exist "'among the brethren, so long as they are instructed "'in these conditions, so long may the brethren be "'expected not to decline, but to prosper.

"'Other seven conditions of welfare will I teach "'you, O brethren. Listen well and attend, and I "'will speak.'

"And on their expressing their assent, he spake as "follows:

"'So long as the brethren shall be full of faith, "'modest in heart, afraid of sin, full of learning, "'strong in energy, active in mind, and full of wisdom, "'so long may the brethren be expected not to decline, "'but to prosper.

"'So long as these conditions shall continue to exist "'among the brethren, so long as they are instructed "'in these conditions, so long may the brethren be "'expected not to decline, but to prosper.'

---

[1] This is an interesting analogue to Philippians iii 13 "I count not myself to have apprehended but this one thing I do, forgetting those things which are behind, and reaching forth unto those things which are before, I press toward the mark."

"'Other seven conditions of welfare will I teach "'you, O brethren. Listen well and attend, and I "'will speak.'

"And on their expressing their assent, he spake as "follows:

"'So long as the brethren shall exercise themselves "'in the seven-fold higher wisdom, that is to say, in "'mental activity, search after truth, energy, joy, "'peace, earnest contemplation, and equanimity of "'mind, so long may the brethren be expected not to "'decline, but to prosper.

"'So long as these conditions shall continue to exist "'among the brethren, so long as they are instructed "'in these conditions, so long may the brethren be "'expected not to decline, but to prosper.

"'Other seven conditions of welfare will I teach "'you, O brethren. Listen well and attend, and I "'will speak.'

"And on their expressing their assent, he spake as "follows:

"'So long as the brethren shall exercise themselves "'in the seven-fold perception due to earnest thought, "'that is to say, the perception of impermanency, of "'non-individuality, of corruption, of the danger of "'sin, of sanctification, of purity of heart, of Nirvāna, "'so long may the brethren be expected not to decline, "'but to prosper.

"'So long as these conditions shall continue to exist

"'among the brethren, so long as they are instructed "'in these conditions, so long may the brethren be "'expected not to decline, but to prosper.

"'Six conditions of welfare will I teach you, O "'brethren. Listen well and attend, and I will speak.'

"And on their expressing their assent, he spake as "follows:

"'So long as the brethren shall persevere in kind- "'ness of action, speech and thought, amongst the "'saints, both in public and in private—so long as "'they shall divide without partiality, and share in "'common with the upright and the holy, all such "'things as they receive in accordance with the just "'provisions of the order, down even to the mere con- "'tents of a begging bowl—so long as the brethren "'shall live among the saints in the practice, both in "'public and in private, of those virtues which (un- "'broken, intact, unspotted, unblemished) are produc- "'tive of freedom[1] and praised by the wise; which "'are untarnished by the desire of future life, or by "'the belief in the efficacy of outward acts;[2] and

---

[1] Buddhaghosa takes this in a spiritual sense. "These virtues "are bhujissāni because they bring one to the state of a free man "by delivering him from the slavery of craving"

[2] The commentator says. "These virtues are called aparāmat- "thāni because they are untarnished by craving or delusion, and "because no one can say of him who practises them, 'You have "'been already guilty of such and such a sin.'' Craving is here the hope of a future life in heaven, and delusion the belief in the

"'which are conducive to high and holy thoughts—so "'long as the brethren shall live among the saints, "'cherishing, both in public and in private, that noble "'and saving faith which leads to the complete de- "'struction of the sorrow of him who acts according "'to it—so long may the brethren be expected not to "'decline, but to prosper.

"'So long as these conditions shall continue to exist "'among the brethren, so long as they are instructed "'in these conditions, so long may the brethren be "'expected not to decline, but to prosper.'

"And whilst the Blessed One stayed there at Rāga- "gaha on the Vulture's Peak, he held that comprehen- "sive religious talk with the brethren on the nature of "upright conduct, and of earnest contemplation, and "of intelligence: 'Great is the fruit, great the advan- "'tage of earnest contemplation when set round with "'upright conduct. Great is the fruit, great the advan- "'tage of intellect when set round with earnest con- "'templation. The mind set round with intelligence "'is freed from the great evils, that is to say, from "'sensuality, from individuality, from delusion, and "'from ignorance.'"

This last paragraph is spoken of as if it were a well-known summary, and it is constantly repeated afterwards in the same Sutta The word I have rendered

efficacy of rites and ceremonies (the two nissayas), which are condemned as unworthy inducements to virtue "earnest contemplation" is samādhi, which occupies in the Pāli Piṭakas very much the same position as faith does in the New Testament; and this section shows that the relative importance of samādhi paññā and sīla played a part in early Buddhism just as the distinction between faith, reason and works, did afterwards in Western theology. It would be difficult to find a passage in which the Buddhist view of the relation of these conflicting ideas is stated with greater beauty of thought, or equal succintness of form.

What would happen to the Society after Gotama's death, formed the subject of a conversation recorded in the same book as having taken place a few days before his death between him and Ānanda, his beloved disciple and constant personal attendant, the St. John, as Moggallāma is the St. Peter, and Sāriputta the St. Paul, of the Buddhist narratives.

"Now when the Blessed One had thus entered upon "the rainy season, there fell upon him a dire sickness, "and sharp pains came upon him, even unto death. "But the Blessed One, mindful and self-possessed, "bore them without complaint.

"Then this thought occurred to the Blessed One: "'It would not be right for me to pass away from "'existence without addressing the disciples, without "'taking leave of the order. Let me now, by a strong "'effort of the will, bend this sickness down again, "'and keep my hold on life till the allotted time be "'come.'

"And the Blessed One, by a strong effort of the will, "bent that sickness down again, and kept his hold on "life till the time he fixed upon should come. And "the sickness abated upon him.

"Now very soon after, the Blessed One began to "recover; when he had quite got rid of the sickness, "he went out from the monastery, and sat down behind "the monastery on a seat spread out there. And the "venerable Ānanda went to the place where the Blessed "One was, and saluted him, and took a seat respect-"fully on one side, and addressed the Blessed One, and "said: 'I have beheld, Lord, how the Blessed One was "'in health, and I have beheld how the Blessed One "'had to suffer. And though at the sight of the sick-"'ness of the Blessed One my body became weak as a "'creeper, and the horizon became dim to me, and my "'faculties were no longer clear, yet notwithstanding "'I took some little comfort from the thought that "'the Blessed One would not pass away from existence "'until at least he had left instructions as touching "'the order.'

"'What, then, Ānanda? Does the order expect "'that of me? I have preached the truth without "'making any distinction between exoteric and esote-"'ric doctrine: for in respect of the truths, Ānanda, "'the Tathāgata has no such thing as the closed fist "'of a teacher, who keeps some things back. Surely, "'Ānanda, should there be any one who harbours the "'thought, 'It is I who will lead the brotherhood,' "'or, 'The order is dependent upon me,' it is he who "'should lay down instructions in any matter concern-"'ing the order. Now the Tathāgata, Ānanda, thinks "'not that it is he who should lead the brotherhood, "'or that the order is dependent upon him. Why then "'should he leave instructions in any matter concern-"'ing the order? I too, O Ānanda, am now grown "'old and full of years, my journey is drawing to its "'close, I have reached my sum of days, I am turning "'eighty years of age; and just as a worn-out cart, "'Ānanda, can only with much additional care be "'made to move along, so, methinks, the body of the "'Tathāgata can only be kept going with much addi-"'tional care. It is only, Ānanda, when the Tathāgata, "'ceasing to attend to any outward thing, or to expe-"'rience any sensation, becomes plunged in that "'devout meditation of heart which is concerned with "'no material object—it is only then that the body of "'the Tathāgata is at ease.

"'Therefore, O Ānanda, be ye lamps unto your-"'selves. Be ye a refuge to yourselves. Betake "'yourselves to no external refuge. Hold fast to the "'truth as a lamp. Hold fast as a refuge to the truth. "'Look not for refuge to any one besides yourselves. "'And how, Ānanda, is a brother to be a lamp unto "'himself, a refuge to himself, betaking himself to no "'external refuge, holding fast to the truth as a lamp,

" 'holding fast as a refuge to the truth, looking not " 'for refuge to any one besides himself?

" 'Herein, O Ānanda, let a brother, as he dwells " 'in the body, so regard the body that he, being " 'strenuous, thoughtful and mindful, may, whilst in " 'the world, overcome the grief which arises from " 'bodily craving—while subject to sensations, let him " 'continue so to regard the sensations that he, being " 'strenuous, thoughtful and mindful, may, whilst in " 'the world, overcome the grief which arises from the " 'sensations—and so, also, as he thinks, or reasons, " 'or feels, let him overcome the grief which arises " 'from the craving due to ideas, or to reasoning, or " 'to feeling.

" 'And whosoever, Ānanda, either now or after I " 'am dead, shall be a lamp unto themselves, and a " 'refuge unto themselves, shall betake themselves to " 'no external refuge, but holding fast to the truth as " 'their lamp, and holding fast as their refuge to the " 'truth, shall look not for refuge to any one besides " 'themselves—it is they, Ānanda, among the Bhik- " 'khus (the members of my Society) who shall reach " 'the very topmost height[1]—but they must be willing " 'to learn.' "

---

[1] That is, Nirvāna, Arahatship

One might go on quoting such passages; but our time is limited. I have had only an hour in which to say something of the great Order, the history of which stretches, for more than two thousand years, over the history of many peoples, compared with whose numbers those of England sink away into insignificance. Having to choose what I should omit, I have tried to deal rather with the kernel than the husk, rather with the heart of the matter than its form, rather with the hopes and feelings and affections that gave rise to the Society, and have been its life-blood and its protection throughout its long career, than with the outward phenomena of dress and residence and food, or even of ecclesiastical history, of missions, of church councils, and of the patronage of kings. And I have been the more inclined to do this, since the line of thought pursued in this Lecture has not, so far as I know, been treated of elsewhere, and since there is not the slightest danger of any European ever entering the Buddhist Order. We shall be quite ready, on the contrary, with a short and sharp judgment on the folly and uselessness of abandoning the world.

At the same time I would venture, in conclusion, to hazard the remark, that it may be open to doubt whether the view of life which led the early Buddhists to do so was further off in one direction from the true one, than the complicated competitions, the unworthy social struggles, the eager, craving restlessness, of this Babylon of ours is on the other. And of one thing I am quite sure, that Europeans in Buddhist countries are often misled by ignorance to jump to harsh conclusions from the outward appearances of Buddhism. A European sees a strange-looking native, dressed in curious robes, and almost uncanny-looking from the effect of a closely shaven head, walking slowly along with a fan in his hand. If he follows him to his home under the palm-trees, he will admire the picturesque appearance of the cleanly-swept ground, the flowering shrubs, the quivering silver leaves of the Bo-tree, and the graceful shape of the little Buddhist tope that adorns the enclosure. At the further end there will be the monk's abode, and perhaps a dark chamber containing one or more painted images of the Buddha, before which are stone slabs on which the villagers place flowers from the shrubs outside. The walls and ceilings may be painted in gorgeous colours, not arranged according to modern taste; and the visitor may chance to see a worshipper muttering some unintelligible words before the image. These the on-looker naturally takes to be a prayer to the idol; and he goes away perhaps with a feeling of contempt for the uncouth and lazy priest, and with a comfortable sense of how much superior a white man is to those brown and hatless idolaters, and how much better than theirs are his own ideas and his own education.

Now there is a great deal to be said for the truth of his opinion. But it is not the whole truth. The particular brother of the Buddhist Order of Recluses whom he has met may be indolent, or ignorant, or self-righteous. There are such men to be found in the ranks of the clergy of all religions. But he may be very much the reverse. There is reason to believe that the ancient spirit of the Order is by no means extinct in China and Japan, or even in Tibet. And I know from personal experience that it survives in Ceylon.

Go and talk to the yellow-robed and tonsured recluse —not, of course, through an interpreter, or out of a book of phrases; you must know not only his language, but something of Buddhist ideas; and you must speak with him as man to man, not as the wise to the barbarian. You will certainly be courteous; for whatever else a Buddhist Bhikkhu may be, he will be sure to give proof of courtesy, and to maintain a dignified demeanour. And it will be strange if you do not find a new world of thought and of feeling opening out before you.

I once knew such a man. He would have seemed nothing to a passing observer but a thin and diseased-looking monk, rather mean in stature. When he first came to me, the hand of death was already upon him. He was sinking into the grave from the effects of a painful and incurable malady. I had heard of his learning as a Pāli scholar, and of his illness, and was grateful to him for leaving his home, under such circumstances, to teach a stranger. There was a strange light in his sunken eyes, and he was *constantly turning* away from questions of Pāli to questions of Buddhism. I found him versed in all the poetry and ethics of the Suttas, and was glad to hear him talk. There was an indescribable attraction about him, a simplicity, a high-mindedness, that filled me with reverence. I used sometimes to think that the personal impression of Yātrāmullē Unnānsē might have led me to colour my judgment of him too highly; but Mr. Childers told me, after my return to England, that the dying Buddhist scholar had made a similar impression upon him. We are not likely to have been both mistaken. And throughout the long history of Gotama's Order, its influence over those who had eyes to see, and ears to hear, must have been moulded and guided by many such men as Yātrāmullē Unnānsē, or it would not have been the power that it has been. Whatever we may think of the folly of abandoning the world, let us at least be sure of this, that the teachings of the Buddhist Suttas have not been recorded, the Buddhist Order was not founded, altogether in vain.

## LECTURE VI.

# LATER FORMS OF BUDDHISM.

---

We have now come, Ladies and Gentlemen, to the end of our journey, and I am afraid you will feel how little has been accomplished. I have been able only to touch the fringe of a great subject, to dwell only upon a few phases of it which are of more especial interest from the point of view imposed upon me by the comparative aim of all these Lectures. What has been left unsaid is a hundred times more in extent, and in many directions more interesting perhaps, and more important, than what has been said. But you, who have listened with so kind an attention to my imperfect endeavours, will appreciate, I trust, the difficulties of my task. I suppose there are about fifty thousand discourses and lectures delivered every week in England alone on Christianity. Who shall count the hours that have been devoted during the past 1800 years, in many a University, to the public discussion of what Christianity is, what it means, what it should teach us? The professors have spoken with a kind of authority on their subject to which a Hibbert Lecturer can lay no claim on his. Have they finished yet? Is the question solved? Are we all quite agreed as to the origin, the growth, the history of Christianity? The wisest Doctor in Divinity would find it difficult to give in six hours even a summary of our disputes. How much, then, of Christianity could he explain, and from the comparative standpoint, in that time, to Buddhists, however cultured, however ready to hear?

And the problem of Buddhism is no less difficult, no less immense. The Buddhism of Nepāl and Tibet differs from the Buddhism of Ceylon as much as the Christianity of Rome or of Moscow differs from that of Scotland or Wales. The Buddhism of Mongolia and China is far removed from either of these, and the Buddhism of Japan has peculiarities all its own. The history of Buddhism, therefore, in each of the countries where it was adopted requires separate treatment. It is incorrect to speak, as is so often done, of Northern and Southern Buddhism as the only two great divisions into which Buddhism had been divided. There was a unity in Southern Buddhism; but there has been no such unity in Northern Buddhism. We may talk, indeed, of Northern Buddhisms; but it would be better to keep the Buddhism of each of the northern countries in which it has been adopted separate and distinct, both in our thoughts and in our language.

And even in each country where it has been received, Buddhism, though it has acquired a distinctive colouring from its new surrounding, has by no means remained permanently the same. The Catholic Church of Christianity is wont to boast that it has never changed. But from century to century the men who form the Church have lived under the influence of changing circumstances, of varying ideas, which have made them believe differently from those who lived before them. They may repeat the same form of words, they may hold to the same form of creed, but they repeat the words in a sense not quite the same, they hold the creed so as to lay stress in different proportions on its various parts. So Buddhism also claims never to have changed. The Buddhist Order has adhered, in orthodox countries, to the same Vinaya, has declared its faith in the same Suttas, from the time when the Pitakas reached their present form, more than two thousand years ago, down to to-day. And even in the countries where the Pāli Piṭakas are forgotten, the Buddhists claim to follow the authority of the unchanging words of the Buddha himself; and they would say, in the words of the lines quoted by the Jātaka Book from the Buddha Vaŋsa:[1]

"As a clod, cast up in the air, doth surely fall to
the ground,

[1] Buddhist Birth Stories, p. 18.

"So surely endureth the word of the glorious Buddhas for ever.
"As the death of all things that have life is certain and sure,
"So surely endureth the word of the glorious Buddhas for ever.
"As, when night to its end hath come, the sun shall certainly rise,
"So surely endureth the word of the glorious Buddhas for ever.
"As the roar of the lion is sure when in morn he hath left his lair,
"So surely endureth the word of the glorious Buddhas for ever."

It is a vain boast. The word of the Buddhas may endure, but the minds of men are ever changing. The history of Buddhism from its commencement to its close is an epitome of the religious history of mankind. And we have not solved the problem of Buddhism when we have understood the faith of the early Buddhists.

It is in this respect that the study of later Buddhism in Ceylon, Burma and Siam, in Nepāl and in Tibet, in China, Mongolia and Japan, is only second in importance to the study of early Buddhism. And we owe a debt of gratitude to those who have attempted to set forth the fate of Buddhism in all these countries, to Spence Hardy, Bishop Bigandet, and Alabaster, to Rājendra Lāl Mitra, Korosi, Koppen and Foucaux, to the brothers Schlagintweit and the fathers Huc and Gabet, to Schiefner and Wassilief, to Dr. Eitel, Dr. Edkins and to Mr. Beal. The history of the later fortunes of the Buddhist faith; the differing forms which it has assumed in different minds; the modifications it has undergone in various countries under the influence of ideas foreign, even antagonistic, to itself; the way in which its fundamental doctrines have been overshadowed and destroyed by the persistent notions of Animism, by the growth of erroneous views as to the Buddha and the Buddhas, by the exaggerated importance attached to its mysticism, to its negative teaching,—all this will be of the greatest value in aiding us to understand the progress of religious ideas among mankind, and more especially in illustrating the causes that have been at work in a similar way on the shores of the Mediterranean.

When we remember how fundamentally opposed are the views of life set forth in the Pāli Piṭakas to those set forth in the New Testament, and how different are the characters, the ideas, the habits and customs, of some of the peoples among whom the two religions have been adopted, we can then perceive how instructive is the fact—one of the most curious facts in the whole history of the world—that Buddhism and Christianity have both developed, in the course of fifteen hundred years, into sacerdotal and sacramental systems, each with its bells and rosaries and images and holy water; each with its services in dead languages, with choirs and processions and creeds and incense, in which the laity are spectators only; each with its mystic rites and ceremonies performed by shaven priests in gorgeous robes; each with its abbots and monks and nuns, of many grades; each with its worship of virgins, saints and angels; its reverence to the Virgin and the Child; its confessions, fasts and purgatory; its idols, relics, symbols and sacred pictures; its shrines and pilgrimages; each with its huge monasteries and gorgeous cathedrals; its powerful hierarchy and its wealthy cardinals; each, even, ruled over by a Pope, with a triple tiara on his head and the sceptre of temporal power in his hand, the representative on earth of an eternal Spirit in the heavens!

If all this be chance, it is a most stupendous miracle of coincidence; it is, in fact, ten thousand miracles. And it cannot be objected that the resemblance is in externals only. The principles which bind each of these two organizations together, which give them their recuperative vital power, are also similar. Each of the two Churches claims to be guided by the eternal Spirit, who is especially present in the infallible Head of the Church; each lays peculiar stress upon the mystic sacrament in which the priest reverently swallows a material thing, and by so doing believes himself to become partaker in some mysterious way of a part of the Divine Being, who, during the ceremony, has become incorporated therein. And the most real resemblance lies deeper still,—in the similarity of the conditions under which the similar developements took place. Each had its origin at a time when the new faith was adopted by the invading hordes of barbarian men bursting in upon an older, a more advanced civilization—when men in body, but children in intellect, quick to feel emotion, and impregnated with Animistic fallacies, became at once the conquerors and the pupils of men who had passed through a long training in religious feeling and in philosophical reasoning. Then do we find that strange mixture of speculative acuteness and emotional ignorance; of earnest devotion to edification, and the blindest confidence in erroneous methods; of a real philanthropy, and a priestly love of power; of unhesitating self-sacrifice, and the most selfish struggles for personal pre-eminence, which characterize the early centuries of Roman Catholicism and of Tibetan Lāmaism alike.

Those who prefer to adhere to the New Testament in the one case, or the Pāli Suttas in the other, are sometimes apt to look only at the worse side of all this, and to regard, therefore, the whole movement of Roman Catholicism, or of Tibetan Lāmaism, with aversion and contempt. But it is no slight merit to have rescued nations from barbarism. And in the long history of the gradual developement of what, in Buddhism, is called the Greater Vehicle, it was the Society, the Church, that instigated or encouraged all that was truest and best in the countries where it prevailed. Those who look only for historical sequences, can watch the centuries, as they pass before their minds, with an unshaken equanimity, a full impartiality; and can recognize—with a kind of awe that fosters sympathy—how insignificant is the individual, how irresistible are the forces working in him and around him, how certainly will similar causes work out, even in the midst of the greatest differences, similar results.

It would be a worthy subject for a future course of Hibbert Lectures to trace out in detail, and with all necessary qualifications, this marvellous parallel. I can only venture here on two remarks—the first in justification of my own choice of subject, the second in protest against a way in which the subject of later Buddhism is sometimes treated.

It is impossible rightly to understand any one phase of later Buddhism in any country, without starting from the standpoint of the earlier Buddhism of the Pāli Pitakas. No one can write the history of later Buddhism, say in Siam or in China, without being thoroughly acquainted with the Pāli Suttas. The very interest of the later inquiries lies in the causes that have produced the manifold changes that they will disclose. We must know not only into what, but also from what, the changes have taken place. This is really a truism; and in the parallel history, with which we are so much more familiar, would be undisputed. A Buddhist, for instance, would never understand Spanish Christianity unless he traced it up, in a manner reasonably and sufficiently complete, from the earliest Church. No other method would keep him safe from constant misinterpretations of the phenomena he saw around him, of the very meaning of the literature on which he would rely.

And, secondly, the whole value of the inquiries into later Buddhism will be lost if they be directed to a purpose which they cannot be reasonably expected to serve. What should we say of a Buddhist, were he to use the writings of St. Augustine as a source from which he might ascertain the opinions of St. Paul, and not as a source of evidence of how those opinions had been, by the time of Augustine, developed? What would be the use of a book in which the opinions of Christ were set forth as obtained from the tomes of Calvin? or, allow me to add, from the sermons of some eminent divine of the nineteenth century in England? In the same way we must not expect to find the teachings of Gotama quite unadulterated in the speculations of some Chinese worthy who lived five hundred years after the Christian era, that is to say, a thousand years after Gotama was born. And if we want to investigate the opinions of early Buddhists, we must not use, as our source of evidence, the very interesting Sanskrit or Tibetan writings of Nepalese or Tibetan Doctors of the Law.

---

If, for instance, you want to have a thoroughly erroneous and unreliable view of early Buddhism, let me recommend to your perusal a much-praised work by M. Barthelemy St. Hilaire, entitled, "Le Bouddha "et sa Religion." This is almost entirely based on a French translation, through the Tibetan, of a Sanskrit work called the Lalita Vistara—a poem of unknown date and authorship, but probably composed in Nepāl, and by some Buddhist poet who lived some time between six hundred and a thousand years after the birth of the Buddha. As evidence of what early Buddhism actually was, it is of about the same value as some mediæval poem would be of the real facts of the Gospel history; and when used for the purposes for which M St. Hilaire has used it, its very real value, as evidence of Nepalese beliefs at the time when it was composed, is lost sight of and forgotten.

This question of the authority of the Lalita Vistara is so important, the work is so often referred to as decisive on questions of early Buddhism, that every one who is reading books on the subject will do well to ascertain and bear in mind what is known about its date.

M. Foucaux has stated, and it has constantly been repeated after him, that it was one of the books received into the canon by the Council held under the Buddhist king Kanishka, about a hundred years after Christ. Now the sole account we have of that Council, our sole authority for what took place at it, is derived from the travels of the famous Chinese pilgrim Hiuen Thsang, who visited India some hundreds of years afterwards. And even he neither mentions the Lalita Vistara in connection with the Council, nor does he say that any canon of sacred writings was settled at the Council; nor is there, indeed, any evidence of the existence of any canon of Buddhist Scriptures at all, other than the Pāli one, till many centuries later.

Whence, then, the idea that the Lalita Vistara was included in a canon by that Council? It is true that the Pāli chroniclers affirm that the Pāli Piṭakas were rehearsed at Asoka's Council, which was held at about the year 250 B.C. at Patna. But what kind of certainty can be given to the argument that therefore those who held Kanishka's Council 350 years afterwards would probably rehearse their sacred books, that those books would probably be in Sanskrit, and that among those books the Lalita Vistara would probably be included? The chain of an argument is only as strong as its weakest link; when all its links are as weak as these, it is wiser to leave it alone, and turn to some evidence a little more reliable.

This we have in the fact that the Lalita Vistara has been translated. We have the original text in an edition published in Calcutta; and on comparing it with the Gya Cher Rol Pa, the Tibetan work which, as above referred to, has been published with a complete French translation by M. Foucaux—the most competent scholar in Europe for the task—we find that the two agree. The Tibetan, as judged by M. Foucaux's version, is in all substantial respects what we understand by an exact translation of the Sanskrit as edited by Rājendra Lāl Mitra for the Bibliotheca Indica. Now M. Foucaux assigns the Tibetan version to some date, which cannot be earlier, but may be much later, than the sixth century of our era, or a thousand years after the birth of Gotama. Here, then, we are on firm ground. Whatever the correct date of the Tibetan version may turn out to be, it will be conclusive evidence of the existence of the Lalita Vistara at that date. The moment we leave this point, however, we come into difficulty.

Thus, for instance, the learned translator goes on to argue, from the existence of four Chinese translations, dating at intervals of a century or so earlier, of works whose original titles were similar in meaning to that of the Lalita Vistara, that our present Sanskrit work with that title is necessarily older than those translations. But it is surely essential first to ascertain whether they were really translations of the same work. This has not yet been done; and until it has been done we have no external evidence which would justify the assignment of the Lalita Vistara to any date earlier than the uncertain one of its Tibetan version. All that we can at present say is, that books of a similar character were in existence as early as six or seven hundred years after the birth of Gotama, and that one of these may turn out to be substantially the same as ours.

Even this hope is founded on the fact that two of these Chinese works, themselves so much later than early Buddhism, consist of chapters whose names in Chinese correspond in meaning to the Sanskrit names of the chapters of the Lalita Vistara. Now when two books on the same subject are divided into the same number of chapters, with practically identical titles, one would naturally suppose that the two works must be the same. That is, however, unfortunately by no means certain. Mr. Beal, to whose labours in these fields of inquiry we owe almost the whole of our knowledge, has translated from the Chinese a work to which he gives the English title of the "Dhammapada "from the Buddhist Canon." The Chinese title is Fa Khieu Pi Hu; that is, "Parables connected "with the Book of Scripture Texts;"[1] and there is a well-known book in the Pāli Pitakas called the Dhamma-padaŋ, or Collection of Dhamma-verses, that is,

[1] So Mr. Beal's "Introduction," p 21.

Verses found in the Dhamma books, or Verses relating to the Dhamma. Mr. Beal, by the title he has chosen for his abstract of the Chinese Text, conveys the impression that the Chinese work and the Pāli one are the same. The opening words of his Preface are: "There are four principal copies of Dhammapada in "Chinese;" he calls the Chinese books generally "faithful versions of works everywhere known in "India," and this particular work a "version of the "Dhammapada." The Chinese work, too, has thirty-nine chapters; and of these, twenty-six have titles which (in meaning) are the same, or very nearly the same, as the titles of the twenty-six chapters into which the Pāli work is divided. And yet, in spite of all this, the two works are essentially different! They are written on a different plan; the Chinese is evidently much later (probably some centuries later) than the Pāli one; and though a few of the verses chosen, from the Dhamma books, for insertion in the Dhammapadaŋ, recur, in a more or less mangled shape, in the course of the stories constituting the Fa Khieu Pi Hu, the great bulk of the earlier work is not found in the later one, and the great bulk of the later work is not found in the earlier one.[1]

---

[1] Of course none of the Introductory Stories occur in the Pāli book, and as regards the verses themselves, the correctness of what I have said will appear from the following analysis, which is arranged for purposes of comparison in parallel columns The verses found

The two books are about as much, and about as little, alike as two modern hymn-books; and to call the later Chinese work "The Dhammapada," is very much the same as if a publisher were to call a volume

---

in the Pāli work are placed in the first column when they recur in the Chinese work, the second column giving the page of Mr. Beal's translation of the Chinese work where similar verses occur in it

| Dhammapada. | Fa Khieu Pi Hu | Dhammapada | Fa Khieu Pi Hu. |
|---|---|---|---|
| 1 | 63 | 107 | 87 |
| 2 | 64 | 108 | 89 |
| 11 | 64 | 109 | 90 |
| 12 | 65 | 127 | 93 |
| 13 | 65 | 128 | |
| 14 | 66 | 137 | 95 |
| 16 | 67 | 138 | 95 |
| 17 | 67 | 139 | 96 |
| 43 | 73 | 140 | 96 |
| 44 | 75 | 141 | 97 |
| 45 | 75 | 212 | 119 |
| 46 | 75 | 213 | 119 |
| 54 | 76 | 214 | 119 |
| 58 | 76 | 218 | 120 |
| 59 | 76 | 229 | 122 |
| 62 | 77 | 230 | 122 |
| 63 | 77 | 243 | 125 |
| 64 | 77 | 259 | 127 |
| 65 | 78 | 260 | 126 |
| 67 | 78 | 261 | 126 |
| 80 | 79 | 264 | 127 |
| 81 | 79 | 265 | 127 |
| 82 | 80 | 270 | 127 |
| 96 | 81 | 324 | 145 |
| 97 | 81 | 326 | 146 |
| 98 | 82 | 338 | 148 |
| 99 | 82 | 383 | 163 |

of religious tales containing about one-seventh of the hymns included in that well-known and much-respected work, by the distinctive title of "Hymns Ancient and Modern." Both the likeness and the difference between two such books and between these two Buddhist books would be due to causes of a similar kind. The Pāli work and the Chinese one are alike because the Chinese one is derived from some work descended from an ancestry related to the Pāli one; and it is different because it is the outcome of a different school, and gives expression to a belief which, though originally the same, has passed through various stages of modification, which have made it essentially different.

Chinese works bearing similar titles, and even divided into chapters bearing similar titles, are not necessarily, therefore, "translations" of any Indian work with a like name. I am quite aware that there are Chinese works that are translations of Indian ones; but no Chinese work has yet been published which is a translation of any Indian work, whether Sanskrit or Pāli, known to us. All that I ask for is greater care in speaking of Chinese works as "the same" as their

| Dhammapada. | Fa Khieu Pi Hu. | Dhammapada. | Fa Khieu Pi Hu. |
|---|---|---|---|
| 384 | 163 | 394 | 164 |
| 393 | 163 | 410 | 164 |

Total, 58 verses, out of a total in the Pāli Dhammapada of 423, recurring (some of them much changed) in the corresponding chapters of the Fa Khieu Pi Hu. See, further, my review in the Academy for August, 1878

Indian prototypes, without sufficient evidence; and I have no doubt that real translations will reward the search of students of Chinese Buddhism, the value of whose labours, and especially of those of Mr. Beal, every one will be anxious to acknowledge as beyond dispute.

This argument will have appeared long. It will not have been too long if it has made clear to you with what difficulties the attempt to give a detailed account of the curious history of later Buddhism must at present be beset. It has seemed to me far preferable, in the few hours allotted to me, to discuss those parts of Buddhism which are comparatively so certain, than to occupy your time with such discussions as this one about the Lalita Vistara, where the details are intricate, and the result not only doubtful, but affording little ground for useful comparisons. I cannot but think, indeed, that any useful discussions of any of the numerous later forms of Buddhism will be impossible till we arrive at an accurate understanding, a more complete consensus of opinion, regarding the earliest Buddhism. And I should not have touched upon the literary questions discussed in the last few pages, had it not seemed to me necessary to enter a protest against the careless and much too common habit of using works dating many centuries after the time of the Buddha, as evidence of the opinions or the teachings of Gotama himself.

I would now invite your attention to a fundamental idea of early Buddhism, closely connected with the doctrine of Karma, which want of time in the third Lecture has compelled me to reserve for this last Lecture.

You will have gathered from previous Lectures that early Buddhism, so far as it was an ethical reformation, propounded a rule of life divided into three great divisions. There was a system of lower morality, intended for those who still wished to remain in the world. There was a second system, including the lower, but going beyond it, for those who had entered the Order. And there was the third, and highest, including both the others, but going again beyond them, for those who had entered what is called the Ariyo Aṭṭhangiko Maggo, the Noble Eight-fold Path; that is to say, the system of intellectual and moral self-culture and self-control which culminated in Arahatship.

What we understand by morality is almost confined to the lowest of the three. The desirability of abandoning the world, the consequences of having done so, the pursuits with which the recluse should or should not occupy himself, are considered in the second. Even this second system, much stricter than the first, is called "a mere trifle, only a lower thing,"[1] as compared with

[1] Brahmajāla Sutta, i. 10

the insight and freedom of the Arahat: and the disciple is not to be satisfied with having attained to this lesser aim.[1] The third consists, on the positive side, of the Seven Jewels of the Law, enumerated in the Book of the Great Decease; and on the negative, of the fetters and veils and hindrances which the earnest Buddhist has to break, to remove, and to overcome.[2] Incidentally, I have touched upon several parts of this system of the Noble Path in former Lectures in this course, and you will recollect that its result is the state of the man made perfect according to the Buddhist faith, the state of Arahatship, one side of which is Nirvāna, that is, the extinction, in this life and in this world, of craving thirst and of its consesequences—lust, hatred, delusion and ignorance.

I would just notice, in passing, that it is craving thirst, and not desire, which in the Arahat is said to

---

[1] Book of the Great Decease, i. 7. Compare St. Paul in Phil iii. 13.

[2] A summary of the first, the lowest stage of Buddhist morality, will be found given from the Sigālovāda Sutta in my manual entitled Buddhism, pp 143—148 An outline of the second will be found there, and again above in the Tevijja Sutta, and the third will be fully treated of in the forthcoming work by Dr Morris on The Seven Jewels of the Law See also, on Arahatship, my Lecture on the "Foundation of the Kingdom of Righteousness," published in the Fortnightly Review, No clvi. (and also separately), the translation of the Sutta, so called, in my Buddhist Suttas from the Pāli (Oxford, 1881), and pp 107—112 of my manual, Buddhism (London, 1877)

be extinct. The second division of the Noble Eightfold Path is the cultivation of right desires. It is only the evil desires, the grasping, selfish aims, which the Arahat has to overcome; and those, unfortunately too numerous, writers who place Nirvāna in the absence of desire, are only showing thereby how exaggerated is the importance which they attach to isolated passages and to careless translations.

But the point to which I would more especially invite your attention is one referred to in the passage I read last Tuesday from the Book of the Great Decease. Arahatship is essentially a condition of insight; and we found the insight of the Arahat there divided into seven kinds—insight into impermanency, into non-individuality, into corruption, into the danger of evil-doing, into sanctification, into purity of heart, into Nirvāna. I am afraid that the mere reading of these words conveys but very little insight into the meaning which lies hidden beneath them. Each of them would require at least a whole Lecture to bring out all its original connotation, all that it suggested to a trained Buddhist, and to take away from the ideas which it now suggests to modern Christians all that is inevitably imported into them from the Christian use of the words. Any one present who is interested in practical ethics, apart from creeds, will find these and the other various details of Arahatship worth the trouble of looking into. I can only propose here to say a few words on the first two in this list. What do they mean? Their names are Anicca-saññā and Anatta-saññā, the perception of impermanency and of non-individuality. They are the very first. Without them, the others cannot exist, that is, cannot exist completely. Now it is curious and noteworthy that the very first of the Saŋyojanas, the Fetters which the disciple has to break on the way to Arahatship, is also the doctrine of individuality (Atta-vāda). It follows that we have to do here with a belief the attainment of which is regarded as of primary importance in the Buddhist system of self-culture, or rather with a delusion whose existence in the mind is regarded as incompatible with any advance along the higher life.

And it is not by chance, not unadvisedly, that the foundation of the higher life, the gate to the heaven that is to be reached on earth, is placed, not in emotion, not in feeling, but in knowledge, in the victory over delusions. The moral progress of mankind depends on the progress of knowledge; the moral progress of the individual depends, according to Buddhism, upon his knowledge. Sin is folly. It is delusion that leads to crime. Men used to slay their children, and children their parents. They have grown out of that, and require no special, no extraordinary personal wisdom to abstain from murder and theft. A man ignorant compared with his fellows may practise the Sīlas. But to make any advance beyond the average standpoint, he must get rid of delusions; he must see things as they are, in a way that ordinary people do not; he must grasp ideas beyond the grasp of the average mind. The fool, the dull man, can never be an Arahat. Does this sound very materialistic, very hard? There is many a man, foolish and dull enough in the world's estimation, who gains but little money, and who earns but little social success, whose eyes are nevertheless open to things beyond the ken of the man successful in the world through a hardness of mind that is incompatible with the humility of faith The dullness which prevents the attainment of Arahatship is not what the world calls dullness; and it often blinds the eyes of the cleverest, the most successful among men. The Buddhist doctrine of the necessity of insight was an encouragement, not a warning, to the poor in spirit; and it has analogies very close and very real with St. Paul's doctrine of justification by faith.

But what is this insight which is the entrance to Arahatship? To appreciate the question, we must go back, as usual, to the early Upanishads. The knowledge which in those writings is praised, with a constant reiteration, as the highest of all gifts, the birthplace, the source, of abiding salvation, is the knowledge of the identity between the individual and God, in whom and by whom the individual lives, and moves, and has his being. As for example:

"He is my self within the heart, smaller than a corn

"of rice, smaller than a barley-corn, smaller than a "mustard-seed, smaller than a canary-seed—yea, than "the kernel of a canary-seed! He also is my self "within the heart, greater than the earth, greater than "the sky, greater than heaven, greater than all these "worlds. He from whom all works, all desires, all "sweet odours and tastes proceed, who embraces all "this, who never speaks and is never surprised, he, "my self within the heart, is that Brāhman."[1] And again:

"What I (the worshipper) am, that is he. What "he is, that am I. This has been said by a Rishi: "'The sun is the self of all that moves and rests.' Let "him look to that. Let him look to that."[2]

Such knowledge is better, according to the Upanishads, than all works, than all rituals. The possession of it is their justification by faith. The ever-present sense of union with God inspires their deepest poetry, and must have given a tone to the life of not a few of those ancient thinkers.

How, then, did Gotama deal with this idea? We have the answer in the two perceptions that are the beginning of the insight, the mental grasp of the Arahat.

The first is impermanency. The Arahat must thoroughly realize, first of all, that all things, all beings, are impermanent. To the peasant, the huge mountain

---

1 Chāndogya Upanishad, III. 14.

2 Aitareya Āranyaka, II. 2, 4, quoting Rig Veda, i. 115, 7.

of the Himālaya range, at the foot of which he tills his tiny field, seems fixed, and sure, and lasting. The Arahat must see through this delusion. The great mountain, and the broad earth on which it rests, must convey to his mind no such impression. To him, it must seem, as it really is, a changing, variable, impermanent, unstable thing, whose existence, compared with the long ages of the revolving Kappas (the æons of the world's renovation and dissolution), is only for a day. And he must not harbour in the remotest cranny of his mind[1] a single exception to this invariable rule. To him, no outward form, no compound thing, no creature, no creator, no existence of any kind, must appear to be other than a temporary collocation of its component parts, fated inevitably to be dissolved. And the glamour of the Vedic poetry must not deceive him, the beauty of the figurative language of the Upanishads must not mislead him. The gods are but beings, living under brighter, happier conditions than men. They, too, have forms, invisible to mortal ken; they, too, are compound things, like everything else. Their heavens will be rolled up as a garment, and they themselves shall be dissolved.

But is there not inside the spirit form of the gods, inside the bodily form of men and beasts, some abiding principle, some self, that survives the dissolution of its case, its sheath, and is itself impermanent? The

* Compare Buddhist Birth Stories, p 253

answer of Buddhism is not only that the idea is a delusion, sprung from the impressions received through the five senses, but that this delusion prevents the attainment of full height in the Buddhist scale of righteousness, is the very first thing to be got rid of by any person who wishes to reach up to anything beyond the ordinary morality of man to man.

Perhaps the most frequently quoted and most popular verses in Pāli Buddhist books are these:

"How transient are all component things!
Growth is their nature and decay:
They are produced, they are dissolved again:
And then is best,—when they have sunk to rest!"[1]

And they are explained by an orthodox commentator as follows:

"In these verses the words, 'How transient are
"'all component things!' mean, 'Dear lady Sub-
"'haddā, wheresoever and by whatsoever causes made
"'or come together, compounds,[2]—that is,- all those
"'things which possess the essential constituents (whe-
"'thermaterial or mental) of existing things,[3]—all these
"'compounds are impermanence itself. For of these,
"'form[4] is impermanent, reason[5] is impermanent,

[1] The last clause is literally, "Blessed is their cessation," where the word for cessation, upasamo, is derived from the word sam, "to be calm, to be quiet," and means cessation by sinking into rest.

[2] Saŋkhārā [3] Khandāyatanādayo

[4] Rūpaŋ [5] Viññānaŋ

"'the (mental) eye[1] is impermanent, and qualities[2] "'are impermanent. And whatever treasure there be, "'whether conscious or unconscious, that is transitory. "'Understand, therefore, 'How transient are all com- "'ponent things!'

"And why? 'Growth is their nature and "'decay.' These, all, have the inherent quality of "coming into (individual) existence, and have also the "inherent quality of growing old; or (in other words) "their very nature is to come into existence and to be "broken up. Therefore should it be understood that "they are impermanent.

"And since they are impermanent, when 'they "'are produced, they are dissolved again.' "Having come into existence, having reached a state,[3] "they are surely dissolved. For all these things come "into existence, taking an individual form, and are "dissolved, being broken up. To them, as soon as "there is birth, there is what is called a state; as "soon as there is a state, there is what is called dis- "integration.[4] For to the unborn there is no such "thing as state, and there is no such thing as a state "which is without disintegration. Thus are all com- "pounds, having attained to the three characteristic "marks (of impermanency, pain, and want of any

---

[1] Kakkhuŋ
[2] Dhammā
[3] Thiti.
[4] Bhaŋgo

"abiding principle),[1] subject, in this way and in that "way, to dissolution. All these component things, "therefore, without exception, are impermanent, mo-"mentary,[2] despicable, unstable, disintegrating, trem-"bling, quaking, unlasting, sure to depart,[3] only for a "time,[3] and without substance;—as temporary[4] as a "phantom, as the mirage, or as foam!"

Buddhism sees no distinction of any fundamental character, no difference, except an accidental or phenomenal difference, between gods, men, plants, animals and things. All are the product of causes that have been acting during the immeasurable ages of the past; and all will be dissolved. Of sentient beings, as we have seen in the third Lecture, nothing will survive save the result of their actions; and he who believes, who hopes, in anything else, will be blinded, hindered, hampered in his religious growth by the most fatal of delusions.

Is it not interesting, is it not strange, that this should be the teaching of the religion which numbers

---

[1] Aneccaŋ, dukkhaŋ, anattaŋ See Jātaka, i. 275, and, on the last, Mahāparinibbāna Sutta, i. 10, and Maha Vagga, i. vi. 38—47.

[2] Khanikā See Oldenberg's note on Dīpavamsa, i. 53

[3] Pāyātā, literally "departed." The forms payāti and payāto, given by Childers, should be corrected into pāyāti and pāyāto. See Jātaka, i. 146.

[4] Tāvakālikā. See Jātaka, i. 121, where the word is used of a cart let out on hire for a time only

more adherents than any other religion which has appeared upon the earth? To us it seems devoid of hope. Is it really so? Must we have a belief in some personal happiness that we ourselves are to enjoy hereafter? Is it not enough to hope that our self-denials and our struggles will add to the happiness of others? Surely we have even so a gain far beyond our deserts; for we receive more, infinitely more, than we can ever give. We inherit the result of the Karma of the countless multitudes who have lived and died, who have struggled and suffered, in the long ages of the past. And if we can sometimes catch a glimpse of the glories that certainly lie hid behind the veil of the infinite future, is not that enough, and more than enough, to fill our hearts with an abiding faith and hope stronger, deeper, truer, than any selfishness can give?

I do not know. But there is at least a poetry and a beauty in these things that may open our eyes a little to things we know not of, that may invite us to look into these matters a little further. We can at least rejoice that the cultivated world is beginning to enter upon the fruits of Oriental research in Indian matters, and that the habit of Western historians of considering all things at any distance from the basin of the Mediterranean as beneath notice, and of thus practically ignoring the existence of about two-thirds of the human race, is beginning to be broken through. It would be useless to attempt to predict the measure of the influence which this change of standpoint will eventually have upon our ideas of history: but it may be compared to the results which followed inevitably on the discovery that this earth was not the centre of the universe. And when we call to mind how closely intertwined are religious with historical beliefs and arguments, we may realize in some degree what effect may follow upon the unveiling of a long history of civilization, independent of Egyptian, Jewish or Greek thought; upon the curtain being drawn back from a new drama of struggling races and rival religions, filled with ideas strangely familiar and as curiously strange. It is not too much to say that a New World has been once more discovered by adventurers as persevering as Columbus, and perhaps at present earning as little gratitude as he did from his contemporaries; and that the inhabitants of the Old World cannot, if they would, go back again to the quiet times when the New World was not, because it was unknown. Every one to whom the entrancing story of man's gradual rise and progress has charms peculiarly its own, will welcome the new light; others will have to face the new facts, and find room for them in their conceptions of the world's history—that history which is the Epic of Humanity. Happy are we if the strains of that epic are ever ringing in our ears, if the spirit of that epic is ever ruling in our hearts! An abiding sense of the long past whose beginnings are beyond imagination, and of the long future whose end we cannot realize, may fill us indeed with a knowledge of our own insignificance —the bubbles on the stream which flash into light for a moment and are seen no more. But it will perhaps bring us nearer to a sense of the Infinite than man in his clearest moments, in his deepest moods, can ever otherwise hope to reach. It will enable us to appreciate what is meant by the Solidarity of Man, and will fill us with an overpowering awe and wonder at the immensity of that series of which we are but a few of the tiny links And the knowledge of what man has been in distant times, in far-off lands, under the influence of ideas which at first sight seem to us so strange, will strengthen within us that reverence, sympathy, and love, which must follow on a realization of the mysterious complexity of being, past, present and to come, that is wrapt up in every human life.

# APPENDIX.

# APPENDIX I.

---

## Speech in Parliament in 1530 on comparing Religions in order to discover Truth, referred to above, pp. 4—6.

The speech referred to in the first Lecture was first pointed out to me in Cobbett's Parliamentary History, Vol. I. p 503, by my friend Mr Allanson Picton. It is there taken word for word from an older and anonymous work, now rare, entitled, "The Parliamen-"tary or Constitutional History of England .. by several Hands," of which the second edition appeared in 1762. The speech is so interesting that I need make no apology for quoting it in full, with the context The passage occurs in Vol. III of the earlier work, pp 57 and foll.

"Many Abuses which the Laity received daily from the Clergy "were loudly complained of, and the King, being now willing that "they should be strictly inquired into, referred the Redress thereof "to the Commons in the Parliament Complaints also being made "in that House[1] against exactions for Probates of Testimonies and "Mortuaries, for Pluralities, Non-residence, and against Priests "that were Farmers of Lands, Tanners, Woolbuyers, &c, the Spi-"rituality were much offended at these Proceedings, and when the "Bills for regulating these Exorbitances were brought before the "House of Lords, John Fisher, Bishop of Rochester, made a remark-"able Speech against them. As the Design of these Inquiries is to "preserve an exact Impartiality, we shall give this Speech verbatim;

---

[1] These Complaints were drawn up into six Articles, and are in Fox's Acts and Monuments, Vol. II. p 907 (edit. 1595)

"as it is printed in a small Treatise on the Life and Death of that "Prelate.[1]

"'My Lords,

"'Here are certain Bills exhibited against the Clergy, wherein "'there are Complaints made against the Viciousness, Idleness, "'Rapacity, and Cruelty of Bishops, Abbots, Priests, and their "'Officials But, my Lords, are all vicious, all idle, all ravenous "'and cruel Priests, or Bishops? And, for such as are such, are "'there not Laws provided already against such? Is there any "'Abuse that we do not seek to rectify? Or, can there be such a "'Rectification as that there shall be no Abuses? Or, are not Cler- "'gymen to rectify the Abuses of the Clergy? Or, shall men find "'Fault with other Mens Manners, while they forget their own, "'and punish where they have no Authority to correct? If we be "'not executive in our Laws, let each Man suffer Delinquency, or, "'if we have not Power, aid us with your Assistance, and we shall "'give you Thanks But, my Lords, I hear there is a Motion made, "'that the small Monasteries should be given up into the King's "'Hands, which makes me fear that it is not so much the Good as "'the Goods of the Church that is looked after Truly, my Lords, "'how this may sound in your Ears I cannot tell, but to me it "'appears no otherwise, than as if our Holy Mother the Church "'were to become a Bondmaid, and now brought into Servility and "'Thraldom, and, by little and little, to be quite banished out of "'those Dwelling-Places, which the Piety and Liberality of our "'Forefathers, as most bountiful Benefactors, have conferred upon "'her. Otherwise, to what tendeth these portentous and curious "'Petitions from the Commons? To no other Intent or Purpose, "'but to bring the Clergy in Contempt with the Laity, that they "'may seize their Patrimony. But, my Lords, beware of yourselves "'and your Country; beware of your Holy Mother the Catholic "'Church, the People are subject to Novelties, and Lutheranism

---

[1] The Life and Death of John Fisher, Bishop of Rochester, &c., by Dr Thos. Bailey (12mo, London, 1655, reprinted, 1739)

"'spreads itself amongst us Remember Germany and Bohemia, "'what Miseries are befallen them already, and let our Neighbours "'Houses that are now on Fire teach us to beware of our own "'Disasters. Wherefore, my Lords, I will tell you plainly what I "'think, that, except ye resist manfully, by your Authorities, this "'violent Heap of Mischiefs offered by the Commons, you shall see "'all Obedience first drawn from the Clergy, and secondly from "'yourselves, and if you search into the true Causes of all these "'Mischiefs which reign amongst them, you shall find that they all "'arise through Want of Faith.'

"The same Authority[1] tells us, that this Speech pleased or "displeased several of the House of Lords, as they were diversly "inclined to forward or flatter the King's Designs But, amongst "them all, none made a Reply to it but only the Duke of Norfolk, "who said to the Bishop,

"'My Lord of Rochester, Many of these Words might have been "'well spared, but I wist it is often seen that the greatest Clerks "'are not always the wisest men'

"To which the Bishop replied

"'My Lord, I do not remember any *Fools* in my Time that ever "'proved great Clerks'

"When the Lower House heard of this Speech, they conceived "so great Indignation against the Bishop that they immediately "sent their Speaker, Audley, attended with a Number of the Mem-"bers, to complain of it to the King, and to let his Majesty know "'how grievously they thought themselves injured thereby, for "'charging them with Lack of Faith, as if they had been Infidels "'or Heretics, &c'

"To satisfy the Commons, the King sent for the Bishop of "Rochester to come before him, when, being present, the King "demanded of him, why he spoke in such a Manner? The Prelate "answered, 'That, being in Parliament, he spake his Mind freely in "'Defence of the Church, which he saw daily injured and oppressed

[1] The above mentioned Life of Fisher

"'by the common People, whose Office it was not to Judge of her "'Manners, much less to reform them, and therefore, he said, he "'thought himself in Conscience bound to defend her in all that "'lay within his Power' However, the King advised him 'to use "'his Words more temperately another Time,' which was all he "then said to him.

"But the Injury the Commons thought they had received, by this "reflection, was not so easily digested, for one of the Members, "making Use of the Gospel Doctrine so far, says the Noble Histo-"rian,[1] as to take a reasonable Liberty to Judge of Things, and, "being piqued at the Bishop for laying it all on Want of Faith, "stood up in that House, and spoke to this effect.

"'Mr. Speaker,

"'If none else but the Bishop of Rochester, or his Adherents, "'did hold this Language, it would less trouble me, but since so "'many religious and different Sects, now conspicuous in the whole "'World, do not only vindicate unto themselves the Name of the "'true Church, but labour betwixt Invitations and Threats, for "'nothing more than to make us resign our Faith to a simple "'Obedience, I shall crave Leave to propose what I think fit in this "'Case for us Laiques and Secular Persons to do; not that I will "'make my Opinion any Rule to others, when any better Expedient "'shall be offered, but that I would be glad we considered hereof, "'as the greatest Affair that doth or may concern us

"'For if, in all human Actions, it be hard to find that Medium, "'or even Temper, which may keep us from declining into Extremes, "'it will be much more difficult in religious Worship, both as the "'Path is supposed narrower, and the Precipices more dangerous "'on every side. And because each Man is created by God a free "'Citizen of the World, and obliged to nothing so much as the "'Inquiry of those Means by which he may attain his everlasting "'Happiness, it will be fit to examine to whose Tuition and Conduct "'he commits himself. For as several Teachers not only differing

[1] Lord Herbert's Life of Henry VIII., p. 295.

“‘in Language, Habit, and Ceremony, or at least in some of these,
“‘but peremptory and opposite in their Doctrines, present them-
“‘selves, much Circumspection must be used. Here then, taking
“‘his Prospect, he shall find these Guides directing him to several
“‘Ways, whereof the first extends no further than to the Laws and
“‘Religions of each Man's native Soil or Diocese, without pass-
“‘ing those Bounds The second, reaching much further, branches
“‘itself into that Diversity of Religions and Philosophies, that not
“‘only are, but have been extant in former Times, untill he be able
“‘to determine which is best But, in either of these, no little
“‘Difficulties will occur For, if each Man ought to be secure of all
“‘that is taught at home, without inquiring further, how can he
“‘answer his Conscience? When looking abroad, the Terrors of
“‘everlasting Damnation shall be denounced on him, by the several
“‘Hierarches and visible Churches of the World, if he believes any
“‘Doctrine but theirs. And that, amongst these again, such able
“‘and understanding Persons may be found, as in all other Affairs
“‘will equal his Teachers Will it be fit that he believe God hath
“‘inspired his own Church and Religion only, and deserted the rest,
“‘when yet Mankind is so much of one Offspring, that it hath not
“‘only the same *Pater Communis* in God, but is come all from the
“‘same carnal Ancestors? Shall each Man, without more Exami-
“‘nation, believe his Priests in what Religion soever, and, when
“‘he hath done, call their Doctrine his Faith? On the other Side,
“‘if he must argue Controversies before he can be satisfied, how
“‘much Leisure must he obtain? How much Wealth and Substance
“‘must he consume? How many Languages must he learn? And
“‘how many Authors must he read? How many Ages must he
“‘look into? How many Faiths must he examine? How many
“‘Expositions must he confer, and how many Countries must he
“‘wander into, and how many Dangers must he run? Briefly,
“‘would not our Life, on these Terms, be a perpetual Peregrination,
“‘while each Man posted into the other's Country to learn the Way
“‘to Heaven, without yet that he could say at last he had known
“‘or tried all? What remains then to be done? Must he take all

"'that each Priest, upon Pretence of Inspiration, would teach him, "'because it might be so, or may he leave all, because it might be "'otherwise? Certainly, to embrace all Religions, according to "'their various and repugnant Rites, Tenets, Traditions, and Faiths, "'is impossible, when yet in one Age it were not possible, after "'incredible Pains and Expences, to learn out and number them. "'On the other Side, to reject all Religions indifferently is as impious, "'there being no Nation that in some Kind or other doth not "'worship God, so that there will be a Necessity to distinguish. "'Not yet that any Man will be able, upon Comparison, to discern "'which is the perfectest among the many professed in the whole "'World, each of them being of that large Extent, that no Man's "'Understanding will serve to comprehend it in its uttermost "'Latitude and Signification · But, at least, that every Man might "'vindicate and sever, in his particular Religion, the more essential "'and demonstrative Parts from the rest, without being moved so "'much at the Threats and Promises of any other Religion that "'would make him obnoxious, as to depart from this Way, there "'being no ordinary Method so intelligible, ready, and compendious, "'for conducting each Man to his desired End Having thus there-"'fore recollected himself, and together implored the Assistance of "'that Supreme God whom all Nations acknowledge, he must labour, "'in the next place, to find out what inward Means his Providence "'hath delivered to discern the true not only from the false, but "'even from the likely and possible, each of them requiring a pecu-"'liar Scrutiny and Consideration Neither shall he fly thus to "'particular Reason, which may soon lead him to Heresy, but, "'after a due Seperation of the more doubtful and controverted "'Parts, shall hold himself to common, authentic, and universal "'Truths, and consequently inform himself, what in the several "'Articles proposed to him is so taught, as it is first written in "'the Heart, and together delivered in all the Laws and Religions "'he can hear of in the whole World This certainly can never "'deceive him, since therein he shall find out how far the Impres-"'sions of God's Wisdom and Goodness are extant in all Mankind, "'and to what Degrees his universal Providence hath dilated itself; "'while thus ascending to God by the same Steps he descends to "'us, he cannot fail to encounter the Divine Majesty.

"'Neither ought it to trouble him if he finds these Truths "'variously complicated with Difficulties or Errors, since, without "'insisting on more Points than what are clearly agreed on every "'Side, it will be his Part to reduce them into Method and Order, "'which also is not hard, they being but few, and apt to Connec- "'tion So that it will concern our several Teachers to initiate[1] us "'in this Doctriue, before they come to any particular Direction,[2] "'lest otherwise they do like those who would persuade us to "'renounce Daylight to study only by their Candle It will be "'worth the Labour, assuredly, to inquire how far these universal "'Notions will guide us, before we commit ourselves to any of their "'abstruse and scholastic Mysteries, or supernatural and private "'Revelations, not yet but that they also may challenge a just "'Place in our Belief, when they are delivered upon warrantable "'Testimony; but that they cannot be understood as so indifferent "'and infallible Principles for the Instruction of all Mankind

"'Thus, among many supposed inferior and questionable Deities "'worshipped in the four Quarters of the World, we shall find one "'Chief so taught us, as above others to be highly reverenced.

"'Among many Rites, Ceremonies, Volumes, &c, delivered us "'as Instruments or Parts of his Worship, he shall find Virtue so "'eminent, as it alone concludes and sums up the rest Insomuch "'as there is no Sacrament which is not finally resolved into it, "'good Life, Charity, Faith in, and Love of, God, being such "'necessary and essential Parts of Religion, that all the rest are "'finally closed and determined in them

"'Among the many Expirations, Lustrations, and Propitiations "'for our Sins, taught in the several Quarters of the World in "'sundry Times, we shall find that none doth avail without hearty "'Sorrow for our Sins, and a true Repentance towards God, whom "'we have offended.

"'And, lastly, amidst the divers Places and Manners of Reward

[1] Sic lege for imitate [2] Quer., lege doctrine

"'and Punishment, which former Ages hath delivered, we shall "'find God's Justice and Mercy not so limited, but that he can "'extend either of them even beyond Death, and consequently "'recompense or chastise eternally

"'These, therefore, as universal and undoubted Truths, should, "'in my Opinion, be first received, they will at least keep us from "'Impiety and Atheism, and together lay a Foundation for God's "'Service and the Hope of a better Life Besides, it will reduce "'Men's Minds from uncertain and controverted Points, to a solid "'Practice of Virtue, or, when we fall from it, to an unfeigned "'Repentance and Purpose, thro' God's Grace, to amend our sinful "'Life, without making Pardon so easy, cheap, or mercenary as "'some of them do Lastly, it will dispose us to a General Concord "'and Peace, for, when we are agreed concerning the eternal Causes "'and Means of our Salvation, why should we so much differ for "'the rest? Since as these Principles exclude nothing of Faith or "'Tradition, in what Age or Manner soever it intervened, each "'Nation may be permitted the Belief of any pious Miracle that "'conduceth to God's Glory, without that, on this Occasion, we "'need to scandalize or offend each other. The Common Truths "'in Religion, formerly mentioned, being firmer Bonds of Unity, "'than that any Thing emergent out of Traditions, whether written "'or unwritten, should dissolve them, let us therefore establish "'and fix these Catholic or universal Notions, they will not hinder "'us to believe what soever else is faithfully taught upon the Autho-"'rity of the Church So that whether the Eastern, Western, "'Northern, or Southern Teachers, &c, and particularly whether "'my Lord of Rochester, Luther, Eccius, Zuinglius, Erasmus, "'Melancthon, &c, be in the Right, we Laiques may so build upon "'these Catholic and infallible Grounds of Religion, as whatsoever "'Superstructures of Faith be raised, these Foundations yet may "'support them'

"This Speech was differently taken also by those who were still "Friends or Enemies to the Church of Rome However, the Majo-"rity being of the latter Opinion, a Reformation in Religion was "resolved upon, as far as was consistent with the established Laws "of the Kingdom"

# APPENDIX II.

## Religious Liberty and Toleration as held by the early Budd[illegible]

In support of the allegation in the note to p 4, I annex here some passages which illustrate the views on respect for the opinions of others held generally by Buddhists about two thousand years before religious liberty was advocated by isolated thinkers in Europe

### 1 Brahma-jāla Sutta.

The following words are placed, at the commencement of the Sutta, in the mouth of Gotama. The Sutta is the first in the Dīgha Nikāya, and is probably one of the very oldest statements of the Buddhist Dhamma, or Doctrine, now extant It is still much read, and very popular among the orthodox Buddhists

"Should those who are not with us, O Bhikkhus, speak in dis-
"praise of me, or of the Dhamma, or of the Saŋgha, you are not on
"that account to give way to anger, heartburning or discontent
"Should those who are not with us, O Bhikkhus, speak in dispraise
"of me, or of the Dhamma, or of the Saŋgha, if you were on that
"account to be either enraged or displeased, it is you (not they)
"upon whom the danger would fall, for would you then be able to
"discriminate whether what they had spoken was right or wrong?"

"Not so, Lord!" was the reply

"Should people so speak, O Bhikkhus, you should explain any-
"thing incorrect in what is said as being incorrect, and should say,
"'This is not correct this is not so this exists not among us, is
"'not found in us!'"

### 2 Asoka's Seventh Edict

On Asoka's inscriptions it is sufficient to refer the reader to M. Senart's important work, entitled, Les Inscriptions de Piyadasi, where all the former authorities are quoted. The seventh Edict runs as follows:

"King Piyadasi, beloved of the gods, desires that all the sects "should dwell (at liberty) in all places They all indeed seek "(equally) after the subjugation (of one's self) and purity of heart "though the people are fickle in their aims and fickle in their "attachments. They may pursue, either in part or in whole, the "aim they set before them. And let every one, whether he receive "abundant alms or not, have self-control, purity of heart, thankful-"ness, and firmness of love. That is always excellent."

### 3 Asoka's Twelfth Edict

"King Piyadasi, beloved of the gods, honours all sects, both "recluses and laymen: he honours them with gifts and with every "kind of honour But the beloved of the gods attaches not so much "weight to alms and honours as to (the desire) that the good name "and (the moral virtues which are) the essential part of the teaching "of all sects may increase Now the prosperity of this essential part "of the teaching of all the sects (involves), it is true, great diversity "But this is the one foundation of all, (that is to say) moderation "in speech, that there should be no praising of one's own sect and "decrying of other sects, that there should be no depreciation (of "others) without cause, but, on the contrary, a rendering of honour "to other sects for whatever cause honour is due. By so doing, "both one's own sect will be helped forward, and other sects will "be benefited, by acting otherwise, one's own sect will be destroyed "in injuring others Whosoever exalts his own sect by decrying "others, does so doubtless out of love for his own sect, thinking to "spread abroad the fame thereof. But, on the contrary, he inflicts "the more an injury upon his own sect Therefore is concord the "best, in that all should hear, and love to hear, the doctrines

"(Dhamma) of each other. Thus is it the desire of the beloved of "the gods that every sect should be well instructed, and should "(profess) a religion that is lovely. So that all, whatever their "belief, should be persuaded that the beloved of the gods attaches "less weight to alms and to honours than to the desire that the "good name, and the moral virtues which are the essential part of "the teaching of all sects, may increase. To this end do the minis- "ters of religion everywhere strive, and the officers placed over "women, and the inspectors, and the other officials. And this is "the fruit thereof; namely, the prosperity of his own sect and the "exaltation of religion generally."

There is no record known to me in the whole of the long history of Buddhism, throughout the many countries where its followers have been for such lengthened periods supreme, of any persecution by the Buddhists of the followers of any other faith.

## APPENDIX III.

# PĀLI TEXT SOCIETY.

### COMMITTEE OF MANAGEMENT

*Hon Treasurer*—W W HUNTER, Esq, C I E, LL D

*Hon Secretary*—U B BRODRIBB, Esq, B A, 3, Brick Court, Temple, E C

Professor FAUSBOLL | Dr MORRIS

Dr OLDENBERG | M EMILE SENART

T W. RHYS DAVIDS, *Chairman*

(*With power to add workers to their number*)

*Bankers*—LONDON JOINT-STOCK BANK, Princes Street, E C

A Pāli Text Society has been started on the model of the Early English Text Society, in order to render accessible to students the rich stores of the earliest Buddhist literature now lying unedited and practically unused in the various MSS scattered throughout the Public and University Libraries of Europe

The historical importance of these Texts can scarcely be exaggerated, either in respect of their value for the history of folk-lore, or of religion, or of language It is already certain that they were all put into their present form within a very limited period, probably extending to less than a century and a half (about B C 400—250) For that period they have preserved for us a record, quite uncontaminated by any outside influence, of the every-day beliefs and customs of a people nearly related to ourselves, just as they were passing through the first stages of civilization They are our best authorities for the early history of that interesting system of religion so nearly allied to some of the latest speculations among ourselves, and which has influenced so powerfully, and for so long a time, so great a portion of the human race—the system of religion which we now call Buddhism And in the history of speech they contain unimpeachable evidence of a stage in language midway between the Vedic Sanskrit and the various modern forms of speech in India. The sacred books of the early Buddhists have preserved to us the sole record of the only religious movement in the world's history which bears any close resemblance to early Christianity, and it is not too much to say that the publication of this unique literature will be no less important for the study of history, and especially of religious history, than the publication of the Vedas has already been

When we call to mind the passionate patience with which well-worn and less important studies are pursued among us, it is matter for wonder that a nearly unworked mine, where the nuggets of gold can still be gathered on the surface, should thus far have remained neglected. But there is no endowment of research among us The well-worn studies afford the means of livelihood, and scholars may well be excused for preferring work that brings immediate reward, to embarking in difficult and untried undertakings There has also been hitherto a want of reliable MSS in Europe from which to edit Pāli texts But this difficulty is now very nearly overcome, and during the last few years the number of scholars who have turned their attention to Pāli has considerably increased.

The Society can now therefore look forward to publishing, within a no very distant period, the whole of the texts of the Sutta and Abhidhamma Pitakas Professor Fausboll having completed the Dhammapada, is already far advanced with his edition of the Jātaka Book, the longest of the texts of the Sutta Pitaka, and Dr Oldenberg has the Vinaya Pitaka well in hand. The remaining texts of the Pitakas lend themselves easily to distribution among various editors The project has been most heartily welcomed by scholars throughout Europe, and Professor Fausboll and Dr Oldenberg (when their present undertakings are completed), Dr Morris, Dr. Trenckner, Dr Thiessen, Dr Frankfurter, Dr Hultsch, Professor Ernst Kuhn, Professor Pischel, Dr Edward Muller, Professor Windisch, Professor H Jacobi, M Léon Feer, M. Senart, Professor Kern, Professor Lanman, and Mr Rhys Davids, have already pledged themselves to take part in the undertaking.

It is proposed to include in the Society's series those of the more important of the earlier Jain and uncanonical Buddhist texts which may be expected to throw light on the religious movement out of which the Pitakas also arose.

Analyses in English of the published Texts, Introductions to them, Catalogues of MSS., Indices, Glossaries, and Notes and Queries on early Buddhist History, will appear from time to time in the Society's Journal

Later on, the Society hope also to publish Translations of all the texts not elsewhere translated. But the series of translations from the Sacred Books of the East, now being published at Oxford under the editorship of Professor Max Muller, has already found room for a version of the greater part of the Vinaya Pitaka, and will find room for others The Society desires to be strictly subservient to that series, and will only deal, in the way of translation, with those books which do not appear in the Sacred Books of the East

The twenty-six books of the Sutta and Abhidhamma Pitakas are written in the Ceylon manuscripts on about 4000 palm-leaves The Vinaya Pitaka, as edited by Dr Oldenberg, will be printed on about 1600 pages 8vo, and it occupies about 900 similar palm-leaves About 7000 pages 8vo ought therefore to be sufficient for the whole of the work, and the cost of printing this quantity of Pāli text in Roman characters will be about £1750

It is proposed to raise the sum in two ways In the first place, the Subscription to the Society will be One Guinea a year, or Five Guineas for six years, due in advance. No charge will be made for postage; and this payment will entitle the subscriber to a copy of all those publications of the Society published during the year for which he subscribes. In the second place, it is hoped that persons who are desirous to aid the objects of the Society and who do not require to receive its publications, will give Donations, to be spread, if necessary, over a term of years. Though the Society has only just been started, a very encouraging number of subscribers have already come forward, including many of the leading Orientalists and University Libraries in Europe, and this number will doubtless increase as the Society becomes better-known But although enough funds are already in hand to enable the Society to go to press with the first volume (which will appear early next year), it cannot hope to be able to depend entirely upon subscriptions A number of donations, varying in amount from five to a hundred pounds, have already been paid or promised, but about £900 more, reckoning each present subscription at ten years' value, will be required if the undertaking is to be carried out to a successful accomplishment Seeing that the distinguished scholars whose names appear in the above list are willing to work without pecuniary reward of any kind, it would be nothing less than a disgrace if such an object were allowed to fall through, in so wealthy a country as England, for so small an amount

As the price to non-subscribers will be about double the amount of the subscription, all intending subscribers are requested to send their subscription at once to the Honorary Secretary, with whom intending donors are respectfully urged to communicate without delay. Bis dat qui cito dat

The following gentlemen have kindly consented to act as agents for the receipt of subscriptions

*Berlin*—Professor Oldenberg (Genthiner Strasse, No 38)
*Paris*—M. Ernest Leroux (Rue Bonaparte, No 28)
*Ceylon*—E. R. Gunaratna, Esq (Attapattu Mudaliyar, Galle)
*Burma*—J A. Bryce, Esq (or in his absence, Henry Maxwell, Esq ), Rangoon.
*Siam*—Henry Alabaster, Esq, Bangkok
*America*—Professor Lanman, Harvard University

The principal contents of the first volume will be selected from the Thera- and Therī-gāthā by Prof Oldenberg, the Ācāranga Sutta by Prof. Jacobi, the Mūla- and Khudda-sikkhā by Dr Edward Muller, the Dīgha Nikāya by Dr Morris and Mr Rhys Davids, and the Anguttara Nikāya by Dr Morris Prof Windisch has undertaken the Itivuttakaŋ, Prof. Kern the Jātakamālā, and Prof. Lanman the Visuddhi-magga

## APPENDIX IV

---

### References to Re-birth as an Animal in the Pāli Suttas.

In the Book of the Great Decease, i 8, 9, 10, Gotama is said to have described to Ānanda a so-called Mirror of Truth, which, if an elect disciple possess, he can predict of himself that re-birth as an animal, or as a ghost, or in any place of woe, is rendered impossible for him. The Mirror of Truth is consciousness of faith in the Buddha, the Dhamma, and the Saŋgha , and the whole doctrine is allied to the Christian doctrine of the final perseverance of the saints

The Pañca-gatiyo, or Five States into which the unconverted man can be re-born, are purgatory, the animal kingdom, and the condition of ghosts, gods and men These Five States are referred to in several passages of the Suttas.

In the first Vagga or Chapter of the Sotāpatti-saŋyutta of the Saŋyutta Nikaya occurs the following passage ·

"What though a king of kings, O Bhikkhus, who has exercised "rule and sovereignty over the four continents, on the dissolution "of the body, after death, be re-born into a happy state in heaven, "into a state of union with the Tāvatiŋsa Gods And there, in the "Grove of Delight, surrounded by crowds of houris, should pass his "time in the possession and enjoyment of the five pleasures of sense "If he be not possessed also of the Four Qualities, he is not set free "from (re-birth in) purgatory, or in the animal race, or as a ghost "He is not delivered, I say, from (re-birth in) evil states

"And what though a disciple who has entered upon the Excellent "Way (an Ariya-sāvako) live upon morsels of food and in much "poverty. If he be possessed of the Four Qualities, he is set free "from purgatory, and from life as an animal or a ghost He is set "free, I say, from (re-birth in) states of woe

"And what are these Four Qualities? They are faith in the "Buddha, in the Dhamma, and in the Saŋgha, and the practice of "those virtues which are unbroken, intact, unspotted, unblemished, "which make men free, and are praised by the wise, which are "untarnished (by the desire after a future life, or by a belief in the "efficacy of outward acts), and which are conducive to high and "holy thoughts"

The last clause is one of the stock descriptions of the higher life of the morality of the Noble Path Compare the Book of the Great Decease, i 11, above, p 31

# APPENDIX V.

## Origen on Metempsychosis.

I am indebted to my father for the following note on Origen's references to Metempsychosis.

Palladius of Cæsareia, who suffered martyrdom A.D. 309, in his "Apology for Origen," which, with the exception of a few fragments, only survives in a translation made by Rufinus of Aquileia (died A.D. 410), thus explains the position taken up by the great Alexandrian upon the subject:

"The most recent charge is that of μετενσωμάτωσις (trans-
"incorporation), that is, the transmutation of souls. To which,
"as we have done with regard to other charges, we will reply in
"his own words." He then quotes Origen as saying, "But these
"things, so far as we are concerned, are not dogmata but spoken
"of for the sake of discussion, and that they may be rejected,"[1]

---

[1] E.g. in Migne, Patrol. Graec. xvii 608, and Routh, Relig. Sacr. iv 383. The passage is probably taken from his De Principiis, i. 8, in Migne, u. s. xi, Rufinus's translation of which is thus rendered by Dr. Crombie in the Anti-Nicene Christian Library, x. 70: "We think that those views are by no means to be "admitted which some are wont unnecessarily to advance and maintain, viz. that "souls descend to such a pitch of abasement that they forget their rational nature "and dignity, and sink into the condition of irrational animals, either large or "small, and in support of these assertions they generally quote some pretended "statements of Scripture, such as, that a beast, to which a woman has unnaturally "prostituted herself, shall be deemed equally guilty with the woman, and shall be "ordered to be stoned, or that a bull which strikes with its horns shall be put to "death in the same way, or even the speaking of Balaam's ass, when God opened "its mouth, and the dumb beast of burden, answering with human voice, reproved "the madness of the prophet. All of which assertions we not only do not receive, "but, as being contrary to our belief, we refute and reject." The original Greek

and proceeds to allege four other passages from his writings in proof that he really held them to be false

1 From Origen's seventh book on the Gospel according to Matthew "Some, indeed, have been of the opinion that the soul "of Elias was the same as that of John, because it is said He is "Elias which was to come For since he said He is Elias, "they thought that it could not be referred to anything else than "his soul; and, from this saying alone almost, they brought in the "dogma of μετενσωμάτωσις, that is, the transmutation of souls, as if "Jesus himself were confirming this But it ought to have been "seen that, if this were true, something similar should be found "in many writings of the Prophets and the Gospels as well. ... "It should be added that, according to what they think, the trans-"mutation of souls takes place because of sins, for what sins was "the soul of Elias transmuted into John, whose birth was predicted "by the very angel by whom that of Jesus was? How then is it "not most evidently false, that he who was so perfect as not "to even taste that death which is common to all, should come "to a transmutation of soul, which according to their allegation "cannot take place except because of sins?"[1]

2 From the eleventh book of the same work, where Origen alleges that the opinion that "souls are passed over from human "bodies into the bodies of animals," to be that of those who are "strangers to the catholic faith," and explains his own to be, "that as it is the virtue of the mind that bestows on any man "that he may become a son of God, so it is evilness of mind ". . that, according to the authority of Scripture, makes any

---

is given by Migne (u s) from a letter addressed by the Emperor Justinian to Menas, Patriarch of Constantinople, A.D 536—552 Rufinus, as usual, translates with great freedom

It is to this passage in the De Principiis that Jerome refers in his letter to Avitus (Ep 124, al 59, c i s f in Migne, Patrol Lat. xxii. 1063), where he quotes Origen much as Palladius has done according to Rufinus. The date of the letter is c. A D 410

[1] C x. in Migne, u.s. 609 This passage only survives in the translation of Rufinus

"one to be called a dog," and that "in like manner are the designations of other dumb animals to be understood"[1]

3 From the thirteenth book of the same work, where, speaking again of the case of Elias, Origen repeats his denunciation of the dogma of the "transmutation of souls," and describes it as "unknown to the Church of God, and one that neither was delivered by an apostle nor anywhere appears in the Scriptures" When commenting upon the saying, He shall go before him in the spirit of Elias, and contending that it was not said in the soul of Elias in order "that μετενσωμάτωσις should have no place"[2]

---

[1] The original Greek is given in Migne, u. s xiii 963, and Routh, u s iv 384 Tertullian discusses the same subject at great length, De Anima, c 32 "Now "our position is this, that the human soul cannot by any means at all be transferred to beasts, even when they are supposed to originate, according to the "philosophers, out of the substances of the elements Now let us suppose that the "soul is either fire, or water, or blood, or spirit, or air, or light, we must not forget "that all the animals in their several kinds have properties which are opposed to "the respective elements There are the cold animals which are opposed to fire ".. In like manner, those creatures are opposite to water which are in their "nature dry and sapless ... So, again, some such creatures are opposed to "blood which have none of its purple hue .. Then opposed to spirit are those "creatures which seem to have no respiration . Opposed, moreover, to air "are those creatures which always live under ground and under water and never "imbibe air . Then opposed to light are those things which are either wholly "blind, or possess eyes for the darkness only .. I maintain that, of which-"soever of the before-mentioned natures the human soul is composed, it would not "have been possible for it to pass for new forms into animals so contrary to each "of the separate natures, and to bestow an origin by its passage on these beings, "from which it would have to be excluded and rejected rather than to be admitted "and received, by reason of that original contrariety which we have supposed it to "possess, . and then, again, by reason of the subsequent contrariety, which "results from the developement inseparable from each several nature"

After some further argument in a similar strain, he concludes by saying " . . "although some men are compared to the beasts because of their character, dis-"position and pursuits, ... it does not on this account follow that rapacious "persons become kites, lewd persons dogs, ill-tempered ones panthers, good men "sheep, talkative ones swallows, and chaste men doves, as if the self-same sub-"stance of the soul everywhere repeated its own nature in the properties of the "animals (into which it passed)" Dr Holms' Transl Anti-Nicene Christian Library, xv 485—487. Tertullian continues the discussion in the following chapter

[2] The original Greek is given by Migne, u.s. xiii 1091 Either Palladius or Rufinus only give the substance of the passage Tertullian ascribes the use of the

4. From his book on the Proverbs "The assertion that souls "are transformed from bodies into other bodies seems to have "occurred to some of those also who appear to believe in Christ, "in consequence of some passages of sacred Scriptures, they not "understanding what is written For they do not observe how a "man may become or made a chicken, or a horse, or a mule, and "they thought that the human soul is transmuted into the bodies "of cattle, just as they thought that it sometimes assumed the body "of a viper" The passage now becomes obscure, but the meaning would appear to be, that this took place just as the devil took the form of a serpent, "which if they say, they ought also to say that "he sometimes takes that of a dragon or a lion"[1]

---

argument derived from the case of Elias to the followers of Carpocrates "whom they so assume to have been reproduced in John as to make our Lord's "statement sponsor for their theory of transmigration when he said, Elias is "come already, and they knew him not, and again, in another passage, "And if ye will receive it, this is Elias which was for to come. "Well, then, was it really in a Pythagorean sense that the Jews approached John "with the inquiry, Art thou Elias? and not rather in the sense of the Divine "prediction, Behold, I will send you Elijah the Tisbite? The fact, "however, is, that their metempsychosis or transmigration theory signifies the "recall of the soul which had died long before, and its return to some other body "But Elias is to come again, not after quitting life (in the way of dying), but after "his translation (or removal without dying), not for the purpose of being restored "to the body, from which he had not departed, but for the purpose of revisiting "the world from which he was translated; not by way of resuming a life which he "had laid aside, but of fulfilling prophecy How, therefore, could John be "Elias? You have your answer in the angel's announcement, And he shall go "before the people, says he, in the spirit and power of Elias,—not "(observe) in his soul and in his body These substances are, in fact, the natural "property of each individual, whilst the spirit and power are bestowed as "external gifts by the grace of God, and so may be transferred to another person "according to the purpose and will of the Almighty" Of the Soul, ii s. 496, 497

[1] Migne, u.s 613 This passage also only survives in the translation of Rufinus In the De Principiis, Origen comments on one of these passages, 1 Cor xv 28, as follows "Since, then, it is promised that in the end God will be all in all, "men are not to suppose that animals, either sheep or other cattle, come to that "end, lest it should be implied that God dwelt even in animals, whether sheep "or other cattle, and so, too, with pieces of wood or stones, lest it should be said "that God is in these also Let us then inquire what all those things are "which God is to become in all. I am of the opinion that the expression, by which

The following passage from Palladius himself on a cognate subject may not be without interest "Some think that bodies "having been prepared and formed in the womb of women, tunc ad "præsem, then immediately souls are created and inserted in the "already formed body, not to say that this cannot be proved from "Scripture—those who hold it do in measure accuse the righteous-"ness of the Creator, because he does not equally assign to all that "is like surroundings of life (æquas vitæ conversationes) For "immediately that the soul was created, when as yet it had com-"mitted no fault, it is inserted, if it so happened, into a blind "body, or one that was otherwise weak, some, moreover (are in-"serted) into healthy bodies, and others into more delicate ones "To some also long time of life is assigned, to others a very short "one, so that sometimes as soon as they were born they were "expelled from the body, and some, moreover, are led into rude "and barbarous surroundings, and where there is nothing human "or honourable, and where an impious parental training is supreme "Some, however, are handed over to honourable men, sober, human, "and where the observation of human laws flourishes, sometimes, "too, to religious parents, where they (have) a noble and an honour-"able education and reasonable instruction

---

"God is said to be all in all, means that He is all in each individual person "Now He will be all in each individual in this way, when all with any rational "understanding, cleansed from the dregs of every sort of vice, and with every cloud "of wickedness completely swept away, can either feel, or understand, or think, will "be wholly God, and when it will no longer behold or retain anything else than "God, but when God will be the measure and standard of all its movements, and "thus God will be all, for there will no longer be any distinction of good and evil, "seeing evil nowhere exists, for God is all things, and to Him no evil is near, nor "will there be any longing or desire to eat from the tree of the knowledge of good "and evil, on the part of him who is always in the possession of good, and to whom "God is all So, then, when the end has been restored to the beginning, and the "termination of things compared with their commencement, that condition of things "will be re-established in which rational nature was placed, when it had no need "to eat of the tree of the knowledge of good and evil, so that when all feeling of "wickedness has been removed, and the individual has been purified and cleansed, "He who alone is the one good God becomes to him all, and that not in the case "of a few individuals, or of a considerable number, but He Himself is all in all" Anti-Nicene Christian Library, x 264, 266, Migne, u s xi 335 et seq

"*Then stronger objection still lies by the opinion that souls are* "the insufflation of the Spirit of God, because it is the substance of "God that sins, if the soul, which is the substance of God, sins, "besides it will be subject to punishment for sin. And if the soul "is created simultaneously with body, it must die so too "If, like other animalia, men spring from seed only, so that the "soul is diffused with the same seed, what shall we say of the "deformed and of abortions? . All souls are of one substance, "and are immortal and rationable, (endowed with) free-will and "choice, that they are to be judged for what they did in this life; "and that they were made by God, who established and created all "things But when they were made, what danger is there in the "opinion that it was all at once of old, or by one by one now?"[1]

---

[1] Apolog for Orig in Migne, n s xvii 604 =Tertullian, De Anima, c. iv, Anti-Nicene Library, n.s. 418, c xxv ib 468

## APPENDIX VI

### Leibnitz and Lessing on Transmigration.

In his Système Nouveau de la Nature,[1] Leibnitz discusses the possibility of life before birth and after death, and says inter alia:

"§ 6 .... Des plus excellents observateurs de notre tems sont "venues á mon secours, et m'ont fait admettre plus aisément que "l'animal, et toute autre substance organisée, ne commence point "lorque nous le croyons, et que sa génération apparente n'est qu'un "dévelopement, et une espéce d'augmentation. . . § 7. Ainsi n'y "a-t-il personne qui puisse bien marquer le véritable tems de la "mort, laquelle peut passer long-tems pour une simple suspension "des actions notables, et dans le fond n'est jamais autre chose dans "les simples animaux temoin les ressuscitations ... Il est donc "naturel que l'animal ayant toujours été vivant et organisé, il le "demeure aussi toujours Et puis qu'ainsi il n'y a point de premiére "naissance ni de génération entièrement nouvelle de l'animal, il "s'ensuit qu'il n'y en aura point d'extinction finale, ni de mort entière "prise á la rigueur metaphysique, et par conséquant au lieu de la "transmigration des ames, il n'y a qu'une transformation d'un même "animal, selon que les organes sont pliés différemment, et plus ou "moins dévelopés"

And then further on, in § 9, he quotes with approval "l'ancien "auteur du livre de la Diète qu'on attribue à Hippocrate, ...

---

[1] Journal des Savans, 27 Juin, 1695 Reprinted in Leibn Opp ed Dutens, Vol ii. Pt i. p 49, and in Leibn. Opp Phil. ed Erdmann, Pt. i. p 124

*Standing Buddha; Mathura, 5th century A.D.*

*Avalokitesvara with Tara and Brikuti (?). Bronze Group consecrated under Queen Didda, later 10th century, Srinagar Museum. (Coutesy Archaeological Department, New Delhi)*

*The Crowned Buddha: Indian Museum; Calcutta,* 1100—1200 A.D.

*Maharaja Lila Manjusri: Indian Museum; Calcutta,* 1100—1200 A.D.

*Stone Temple: Site No. 2: Nalanda*

*Buddha preaching his first Sermon:*
*Sarnath Museum, Gupta Period*

*The Buddha Temple: Bodh-Gaya. Ascribed to Kushan Dynasty. About A.D. 2nd century.*

*Buddhapada: Early Phase*

*The Buddha from Akhnur: Almost life size*

*Buddha head; Early Gupta—Mathura, 5th century A.D.*

"que les animaux ne nourrent et ne meurent point, et que les choses "qu'on croit commencer et périr, ne font que paroitre et disparoitre"

Leibnitz therefore, like Gotama, rejects transmigration only to adopt a theory which allows of pre-existence, and of a connection of cause and effect between different individuals And in Lessing's opinion, as in Gotama's, there is a law of nature which involves continuity of being between different individuals I only know his theory, which is contained in a rare tract entitled "**Dass mehr als funf Sinne fur den menschen sein konnen,**" from the summary given by Professor Goldstucker in his article on Transmigration, contributed to Knight's Encyclopædia Metropolitana, and reprinted in the Literary Remains of Theodor Goldstucker, p 218 He there says

"His arguments are briefly these: The soul is a simple being, "capable of infinite conceptions But being a finite being, it is "not capable of such infinite conceptions at the same time It "must obtain them gradually in an infinite succession of time If, "however, it obtain them gradually, there must be an order in "which and a degree to which these conceptions are acquired "This order and this measure are the senses At present the soul "has of senses five But neither is there any ground to assume "that it has commenced with having five senses, nor that it will "stop there For since nature never takes a leap, the soul must "have gone through all the lower stages before it arrived at that "which it occupies now And since nature contains many "substances and powers which are not accessible to those senses "with which it is now endowed, it must be assumed that there "will be future stages, at which the soul will have as many senses "as correspond with the powers of nature And this my system"—Lessing concludes his essay in a fragmentary note discovered after his death—"this my system is certainly the oldest of all philo-"sophical systems For it is, in reality, no other than the system "of the pre-existence of the soul and metempsychosis, which did "not only occupy the speculation of Phythagoras and Plato, but "also before them of Egyptians, Chaldeans, and Persians—in short, "of all the sages of the East And this circumstance alone "ought to work a prejudice in its favour. For the first and oldest "opinion is, in matters of speculation, always the most probable, "because common sense immediately hit upon it."

## APPENDIX VII

### On Souls going to the Moon.

On the curious belief mentioned above, p. 82, of souls going to the moon, Mr Tylor says, in his Primitive Culture, ii. 69, 70 · "Fourthly, in old times and new, it has come into men's minds "to fix upon the sun and moon as abodes of departed souls When "we have learnt from the rude Natchez of the Mississippi and the "Apalaches of Florida that the sun is the bright dwelling of de-"parted chiefs and braves, and have traced like thoughts on into "the theologies of Mexico and Peru, then we may compare these "savage doctrines with Isaac Taylor's ingenious supposition, in his "Physical Theory of Another Life, that the sun of each pla-"netary system is the house of the higher and ultimate spiritual "corporeity, in the centre of assembly to those who have passed on "the planets their preliminary era of corruptible organization. Or "perhaps some may prefer the Rev Tobias Swinden's book, pub-"lished in the last century, and translated into French and German, "which proved the sun to be hell, and its dark spots gatherings of "damned souls And when in South America the Saliva Indians "have pointed out the moon as their paradise, where no mosquitos "are, and the Guaycurus have shown it as the home of chiefs and "medicine-men deceased, and the Polynesians of Tokelan, in like "manner, have claimed it as the abode of departed kings and chiefs, "then these pleasant fancies may be compared with that ancient "theory mentioned by Plutarch, that hell is in the air and elysium "in the moon, and again, with the mediæval conception of the "moon as the seat of hell,[1] a thought elaborated in profoundest "bathos by Mr. M. F Tupper:

"'I know thee well, O Moon, thou cavern'd realm,
Sad Satellite, thou giant ash of death,
Blot on God's firmament, pale home of crime,
Scarr'd prison-house of sin, where damned souls
Feed upon punishment Oh, thought sublime,
That amid night's black deeds, when evil prowls
Through the broad world, thou, watching sinners well,
Glarest o'er all, the wakeful eye of—Hell!'"

Skin for skin, the brown savage is not ill matched in such speculative lore with the white philosopher.

The Manicheans had a belief which it would be well to compare with the above So Epiphanius (Adv. Hær 66) gives the following as the views of Tyrbo:

"The wisdom of the more than good God, bethinking itself that "the soul diffused through everything, being captive of the princes "and opposite principle and root, was cast into bodies—for its sake[2] ".... placed these lights in the heavens, the Sun, the Moon, "and the Stars—having performed this work by what the Greeks "say are the twelve elements. And the elements, he (i e Tyrbo) "maintains, draw the souls of dying men and other animals, they "being of the nature of light, bear them to a light boat (because he "wishes to call the sun and moon voyages), and the light boat, or "ship, is laden up to the fifteenth day, according to the fulness of "the moon, and so it (the soul) is sent on and set down from the "fifteenth day in the great ship, that is the sun. The sun then "carries them on into the world of life and the region of the blessed. "And thus souls are sent on by the sun and the moon."

And this is confirmed, though with some difference in detail, by the Disputaton of Archelaus, where it is said of the doctrine of Manes:

[1] See Alger, Future Life, p 590

[2] The Manicheans hold the soul to be a part of God (as the Stoics did)

"When the living Father perceived that the soul was in tribulation in the body, He sent his own Son for (its) salvation Then "He came and prepared the work which was to effect the salvation "of the souls, and with that object prepared an instrument with "twelve urns (κάδους), which is made to revolve with the sphere, "and draws up with it the souls of the dying And the greater "luminary receives those souls, and purifies them with its rays, and "then passes them over to the moon, and in this manner the moon's "disc, as it is designated by us, is filled up For he (i.e Manes) "says that these two luminaries are ships or passage boats (πορθμεῖα). "Then, if the moon becomes full, it ferries its passengers across "towards the E wind, and thereby effects its own waning in getting "itself delivered of its freight And in this manner it goes on "making the passage across, and again discharging its freight of "souls drawn up by the urns, until it saves its own proper portion "of the souls

"Moreover, he (Manes) maintains that every soul, yea, every "living creature, partakes of the substance of the good Father And "accordingly, when the moon delivers over its freight of souls to "the æons of the Father, they abide there in that pillar of glory "which is called the perfect air And this air is a pillar of light, "for it is filled in the souls that are being purified."

# APPENDIX VIII

## Plato on the Soul.

As this volume is likely to fall into the hands of readers in the East who may not be able to refer to the passage for themselves, I here add the context of the passage quoted above, pp 95—97, from the Phædo:

"And this is the reason . . . . why the true votaries of philosophy "abstain from all fleshly lusts, and endure and refuse to give them-"selves up to them,—not because they fear poverty or the ruin of "their families, like the lovers of money and the world in general; "nor like the lovers of power and honour, because they dread the "dishonour or disgrace of evil deeds . . . Therefore they who have "any care of their own souls, and do not merely live moulding and "fashioning the body, say farewell to all this, they will not walk "in the ways of the blind; and when philosophy offers them "purification and release from evil, they feel that they ought not to "resist her influence, and whither she leads they turn and follow.

". . . . The lovers of knowledge are conscious that their souls, "when philosophy takes them in hand, are simply fastened and "glued to their bodies the soul is able to view real existence only "through the bars of a prison, and not of herself unhindered; she "is wallowing in the mire of all ignorance; and philosophy, behold-"ing the terrible nature of her confinement, inasmuch as the captive "through lust becomes a chief accomplice in her own captivity,— "for the lovers of knowledge are aware that this was the original "state of the soul, but that when she was in this state philosophy "adopted and comforted her, and wanted to release her, pointing "out to her that the eye and the ear and the other senses are full "of deceit, and persuading her to retire from them in all but the "necessary use of them, and to be gathered up and collected into "herself, and to trust only to herself and her own pure apprehensions "of pure existence, and to mistrust whatever comes to her through "other channels and is subject to vicissitude,—philosophy, I say, "shows her that all her own nature is intellectual and invisible "And the soul of the true philosopher thinks that she ought not to "resist this deliverance, and therefore abstains from pleasures and "desires and pains and fears, as far as she is able, reflecting that "when a man has great joys or sorrows or fears or desires, he suffers "from them, not merely the sort of evil which might be anticipated, "—as, for example, the laws of his health or property, which he "has sacrificed to his lusts,—but an evil greater far, which is the "greatest and worst of all evils, and one of which he never thinks.

"And what it that, Socrates? said Cebes.

"Why, that when the feeling of pleasure and pain in the soul is "most intense, all of us naturally suppose that the object of this "intense feeling is then plainest and truest, but such is not the "case .... And this is the state in which the soul is most en-"thralled by the body[1]. . because each pleasure and pain is a "sort of nail which nails and rivets the soul to the body, until she "becomes like the body, and believes that to be true which the "body affirms to be true, and from agreeing with the body and "having the same delights, she is obliged to have the same habits "and haunts, and is not likely ever to be pure at her departure . .. "but is always impeded by the body, and so she sinks into another "body and there germinates and grows"

---

[1] Rep x. Jowett, iii 516 seq

# APPENDIX IX.

## Further Note on the word Piṭaka.

In connection with the remark on p. 49, as to the use of the word Piṭaka, or Basket, for the Buddhist canon, it has been pointed out to me that Epiphanius of Salamis, the well-known Hæresiologist of the fourth century, entitled his great work Πανάριον, which is the Latin pannarium, originally used of a bread-basket, whence our English pannier. He, however, explains the sense in which he used the word by the addition, "sive capsulam medicum." The parallel is curious and perhaps suggestive.

Schlagintweit informs us, in his Buddhism in Tibet (pp 97, 98) that an image of one of the Buddhist Upāsakas, put up in the monastery of Gyungul, "carries a basket filled with the sheets of a "religious book. . . . . This very ancient mode of using a basket for "the palm-leaves . . . . is said to be still in use in Tibet, the single "volumes of larger works being put together into a common basket" No information is given as to the age of the image, but it is certainly very late, perhaps a century or so old I only quote the passage as evidence of modern Tibetan ideas on the subject

## APPENDIX. X

### Nirvāna.

When, in writing my manual of Buddhism, I was endeavouring to reconcile the apparently discrepant descriptions of Nirvāna which had led some scholars to the conclusion that it meant the annihilation of being or the annihilation of the soul, and others to the contrary conclusion, that it meant the eternal existence of the soul in a state of bliss, and was gradually led to the startling conclusion that Gotama, in his description of Nirvāna, was expressing no opinion at all, either one way or the other, as to existence after death, but was proclaiming a salvation from the sorrows of life which was to be reached here on earth in a changed state of mind, I saw indeed that this explanation would remove all the previous difficulties in the passages then before me, but I little thought that further research in the Pāli Scriptures would disclose any passages in which the misunderstandings of European investigators would be clearly and authoritatively met This has, however, been the case Every day, as new portions of the Pāli Pitakas are being made accessible, fresh confirmation is being afforded to the truth of the view I had ventured to put forward, and Dr Frankfurter has been the first to point out three important passages in the Saŋyutta Nikāya which would be decisive on the point if it were still open to doubt In two of these passages Sāriputta, and in the third Gotama himself, are represented as stating, in answer to a direct question what Nirvāna is, that it is the destruction of passion, malice, and delusion (rāga, dosa, and moha) The context may be seen in Dr Frankfurter's paper in the Journal of the Royal Asiatic Society for 1880, in which the full Pāli texts are given, with summarized translations and notes

# APPENDIX XI.

## The Key-note of the "Great Vehicle."

Had I had time for another Lecture, I should have been glad of the opportunity of enlarging further on the idea of a desire to save all living creatures, quoted above, p. 112, from the Sūtra of the 42 Sections

It is acknowledged that the Great Vehicle, the Mahāyāna, entirely supplanted in Northern India the older Buddhism of the Little Vehicle, the Hīnayāna What was it that gave to the later movement that superior vital power which enabled it to outlive the earlier teaching? Mr Beal, in the Introduction to his Travels of Fa Hian, pp. lvii and foll, places the distinguishing characteristics of the newer school in certain metaphysical subtleties which could scarcely have gained for it the ear of the multitude I venture to think that the idea referred to above, as summarized in the theory of Bodisatship, is the key-note of the later school, just as Arahatship is the key-note of early Buddhism. The Mahāyāna doctors said, in effect "We grant you all you say about the bliss of attaining Nirvāna in this life But it produces advantage only to yourselves, and according to your own theory there will be a necessity for Buddhas in the future as much as there has been for Buddhas in the past Greater, better, nobler, then, than the attainment of Arahatship, must be the attainment of Bodisatship from a desire to save all living creatures in the ages that will come."

The new teaching, therefore, was in no conscious contradiction to the old; it accepted it all, and was based upon it Its distinguishing characteristic was the great stress which it laid on one point of the earlier doctrine to the gradual overshadowing of the rest Its strength lay in the grandeur of its appeal to self-renunciation. It is true the newer school unconsciously changed the centre point of the system, the focus of their mental vision, and the logical consequences of the step they had taken led to the corruption of Buddhism They might have been wiser had they perceived that their duty to the race would have been more completely fulfilled by their acting up to the ideal of Arahatship But it was at least no slight merit to have been led, even though they were led astray, by a sense of duty to the race And readers of the Mahāyāna books, tedious as they have so often been called, will find them acquire a new significance and a new beauty when they are read in the light of this conception.

# INDEX.

The pronunciation of Pāli words is exceedingly easy The vowels have always the same sound as in Italian or German (except that unaccented short a is pronounced as u in but), and the consonants the same as in English (except that c = ch, ñ = ny, and ŋ = ng) The dotted t, d, n, are the same as in English; but the simple d, t, n, are pure dentals,—that is, they are pronounced with the tongue against the teeth. The accent is always on the long syllable For further details, see my manual, Buddhism, p v.

## Misprints.

P 23, for Sudras, read Ṣūdras
P 41, for Pavāranā, read Pavāranā
P. 45, for The Suttas, in the third Nikāya, give the same doctrines, read, The Suttas in the third Nikāya give the same doctrines
P. 49, note, for Brāhman, read Brāhmans
P 53, line 6, after dissolved, insert a comma.
P 93, five lines from the bottom, for serve the moral cause, read, save the mòral cause
P 100, for Nirvana, read Nirvāna
P. 133, for Veluriya, read Veluriya.

## *WORKS BY THE SAME AUTHOR.*

---

### I. Buddhism: being a Sketch of the Life and Teachings of Gotama the Buddha With a Map (Small 8vo, London—Society for Promoting Christian Knowledge. 1878) *Seventh Thousand.* 2s 6d

"We do not know of any other work from which so fair and complete an account can be obtained of that wonderful religion which has so much in common with Christianity, and has numbered more adherents than any other religion in the world"—*Academy*

"Altogether higher stands the little work of Mr Rhys Davids, . written in an agreeable style, and with great knowledge of the facts, . which we should wish to see in the hands of all students of religious history, and hope to see translated into our own language '—*Theologisch Tijdschrift.*

### II. Buddhist Birth Stories, or Jātaka Tales; the Oldest Collection of Folk-lore extant. (8vo, London—Trubner Vol I. 1880) 18s

This is a translation from the Pāli text of the standard Buddhist Collection as edited by Professor Fausböll, and is preceded by an Introduction on the history of the Birth-story literature, and by bibliographical and other tables.

"Among the various contributions to the comparative study of folk-lore, Mr Rhys Davids's translation of the Jātakas must take a foremost place "—*Saturday Review*

"These tales are the nearest representatives of the original Aryan stories from which sprang the folk-lore of Europe as well as of India, and from which the Semitic nations also borrowed much The Introduction contains a most interesting disquisition on the migrations of those fables, tracing their reappearance in the various groups of folk lore legends known as 'Æsop's Fables,' 'The Hitopadesa,' 'The Kalilag and Damnag Series,' and even 'The Arabian Nights' Among other old friends we meet with a version of the Judgment of Solomon, which proves after all to be an Aryan, and not a Semitic tale "—*Times*

"It is certain that no more competent exponent of Buddhism could be found than Mr Rhys Davids, and that these Birth Stories, of which he has now given us the first instalment, will be of the greatest interest and importance to students." *St James's Gazette*

"The translation could not have fallen into better hands. And what is no small merit, when we consider the involved style of Buddhist writings, it is easy to read, though at the same time it is faithful throughout "—*Revue de l'histoire des Religions*

"The English version, while strictly literal, is thoroughly idiomatic It is not too much to say that no Pāli scholar could have been found more competent for the work than he to whom it has been entrusted He has thoroughly entered into the spirit of his original, and his renderings, even of the most difficult passages, are always most accurate and felicitous. In a valuable and interesting Introduction, the translator traces the course of transmigration of the Buddhist stories and fables from East to West—by many and various courses, Hindu, Persian, Arabic, Syriac, Greek—through the Kalilag and Damnag literature down to the so-called fables of Æsop."—*Contemporary Review*

## WORKS BY THE SAME AUTHOR.

**III. Report on the existing European Literature on Pāli** and Siŋhalese in Transactions of the Philological Society, 1875, 1876 (London—Trubner & Co) 6s

"In the Anniversary Address for 1875, Mr Rhys Davids gave us a very interesting and almost complete summary of the work done by Pāli philologists up to that date, leaving very little for any one else to contribute "—*Report of the Philological Society for* 1880

**IV. Buddhist Suttas, from the Pāli.** (8vo; Oxford—Clarendon Press, 1881) 10s

"Mr Rhys Davids's excellent translation."—*Athenæum*

"We thank Mr Rhys Davids for his valuable contribution to the *Sacred Books of the East*, and we trust that we shall not long have to wait for another equally interesting volume of *Buddhist Suttas*"—*Academy*

**V. Vinaya Texts; translated from the Pāli by T. W.** Rhys Davids and Hermann Oldenberg (8vo, Oxford—Clarendon Press Vol. I. nearly ready, Vol. II. in the press; Vols. III. and IV. in preparation.) Nos IV. and V. form part of "The Sacred Books of the East"

**VI. The Ancient Coins and Measures of Ceylon; with** an Introductory Chapter on the Coins and Measures in use in India in the Time of Early Buddhism, and a Supplementary Chapter on the Date of the Buddha's Death (Imp 4to, with a Photo-lithographic Plate, London—Trubner & Co., 1877) 10s

"Throughout the supplementary chapter, as in the whole work, we find acute criticism and extensive learning united with caution in the drawing of conclusions, and not a few incidental observations that are instructive also for a reader not especially interested in this particular branch of numismatic inquiry."—*Journal of the German Asiatic Society*

**VII. Three Inscriptions of Parākrama Bāhu; with fac**simile Plates, the Text in Elu, Translation, and Notes (8vo, London—Trubner & Co, 1874) 1s 6*d*.

**VIII. Sīgiri, the Lion Rock, near Pulastipura, Ceylon:** a Description and Account of the Ruins and Inscriptions there. Together with the Pāli Text of the 39th Chapter of the Mahāvaŋsa, Translation, and Notes (8vo, London—Trubner, 1875) 1s 6*d*

**IX. Two old Siŋhalese Inscriptions. Elu Texts, Trans**lation, and Notes (8vo, London—Trubner & Co, 1876) 1s 6*d*

The above three Essays are reprinted from the *Journal of the Royal Asiatic Society*

# BOOKS IN PALI.

## BUDDHIST SCRIPTURES IN PALI.

In 5 vols 8vo, 21s each Volume,

**The Vinaya Pitakam, one of the principal Buddhist** Holy Scriptures in the Pali Language Edited by Dr. H. OLDENBERG. Vol I. The Mahavagga, with an Introduction Vol. II. The Cullavagga Vol. III. The Suttavibhanga, I. (Parajika, Samghadisesa, Anyata, Nissaggiya) Published with the assistance of the Royal Academy of Berlin, and of the Secretary for India in Council. Vols IV. V in the press.

8vo, cloth, 21s

**The Dîpavamsa, an Ancient Buddhist Historical Record** in the Pali Language Edited, with an English Translation, by Dr. H OLDENBERG

The Dîpavamsa is the most ancient historical work of the Ceylonese; it contains an account of the ecclesiastical history of the Buddhist Church, of the conversion of the Ceylonese to the Buddhist faith, and of the ancient history of Ceylon.

The study of Pali is in India raised to the level of that of Sanskrit, and is made the subject of examination in the University of Calcutta. In the absence of text-books, the "Dipavamsa" is specially adapted for the purpose, on account of the accompanying translation.

8vo, 21s

**The Milinda Pañho. Being Dialogues between King** Milinda and the Buddhist Sage Nâgasena. The Pali Text edited by V. TRENCKNER, of Copenhagen.

Also 8vo, 4s

**Pali Miscellany, by V. Trenckner. Part I. The Introductory** Part of the Milinda Pañho, an English Translation and Notes

"A very interesting dialogue between Milinda and Nagasena"—*Max Müller in Chips, I*

"Next in order of interest should undoubtedly be named the 'Milindha Panha', or, Questions of Menander' Whatever be the origin of this remarkable work, there can be no doubt of its great antiquity, for it exhibits a familiarity with Greek names and places, and records a religious discussion between the Buddhist divine Nagasena, and a 'Yona' king Milinda, who can be identified with certainty with the Bactrian king Menander."—*Childers in Pali Dictionary.*